WINNIPEG
SEP 05 2013
PUBLIC LIBRARY

D1015470

BULLYING

BULLYING

Sally Kuykendall, PhD

Health and Medical Issues Today

AN IMPRINT OF ABC-CLIO, LLC
Santa Barbara, California • Denver, Colorado • Oxford, England

Library of Congress Cataloging-in-Publication Data

Kuykendall, Sally.
Bullying / Sally Kuykendall.
p. cm.—(Health and medical issues today)
Includes bibliographical references and index.
ISBN 978-1-4408-0027-6 (hardcopy : alk. paper)—
ISBN 978-1-4408-0028-3 (ebook : alk. paper)
1. Bullying. 2. Bullying—Prevention. I. Title.
BF637.B85K89 2012
302.34'3—dc23 2012025061

ISBN: 978-1-4408-0027-6
EISBN: 978-1-4408-0028-3

16 15 14 13 2 3 4 5

This book is also available on the World Wide Web as an eBook.
Visit www.abc-clio.com for details.

Greenwood
An Imprint of ABC-CLIO, LLC

ABC-CLIO, LLC
130 Cremona Drive, P.O. Box 1911
Santa Barbara, California 93116-1911

This book is printed on acid-free paper ∞

Manufactured in the United States of America

Contents

Preface ix
Introduction xv

Section I 1

1 Bullying is a Health Issue 3
The Definition of Health 5
How Researchers Study Bullying 7
The History of Bullying Research 9
Major Historical Events and Bullying 15
School Attacks and Bullying 16
Suicides and Bullying 24

2 The Definition of Bullying 31
An Imbalance of Power 32
Purposeful and Chronic 38
Confusion with Other Harmful Behaviors 39
Bystander Behavior 41
Forms of Attack 42
Physical Bullying 43
Verbal and Nonverbal Bullying 43
Psychological Bullying 44

3 Prevalence 47
Differences by Age and Gender 48
High-Risk Groups 49

4 Diagnosis 55
Symptoms of Victimization 55
Symptoms of Perpetration 59

5 Health Consequences 63
Consequences of Victimization 63
Consequences of Perpetration 66
Consequences of Combined Victimization and Perpetration 68
Consequences of Witnessing Bullying 68
Financial Consequences to Schools and Communities 69

6 Causes of Bullying 71
Biological 74
Frustration–Aggression 77
Narcissistic Personality 78
Adolescent Development 79
Violence as a Learned Behavior 81
Moral Development 83
Incongruent Styles of Relating 86
Henchmen: Why Others Obey the Bully 88
Genovese Syndrome 89
Institutionalized Bullying 91
The Community 93

7 Treatment and Prevention 95
Emergency Medical Care 96
Emotional Support of Victims 97
Preventing Further Attacks 99
Healing after the Trauma 102
Developing Supportive Friendships 102
Offender Services 105
Building Empathy 106
Bystanders 109
The Role of Parents 110
Discussing Bullying and Expectations of Behavior 110
Support in Building Positive Friendships 111
Preventing Violence-Related Behaviors 111
Restricted Access to Firearms 113
Limiting Exposure to Media Violence 113
Educators 115
Classroom Management 115
Handling Incidents of Bullying with Dignity and Respect 116

Threat Assessment 119
Evidence-Based Programs 120
Pediatric Health Care Providers 121
Laws 122
Recommendations from the World Health Organization 123
Truth and Reconciliation 124

Section II 129

Controversies and Issues 131

Section III 141

Resources 143

Glossary 147
References 153
Index 161

Preface

At some point in life, just about everyone will meet a bully, a person who has social influence and uses that influence to hurt or control other people. Bullies are everywhere—in schools, workplaces, communities, parks, and shopping malls. They can make life downright miserable. Bullies hurt others by hitting, spreading nasty rumors, name-calling, making inappropriate comments, giving icy looks, or by making others feel unwelcome and unwanted. Bullies enjoy making their victims feel bad because it makes them feel better, bigger, stronger, and more powerful. They use their social power to convince others to join in the attacks, directing henchmen to hurt the victim. Outnumbered and humiliated, the victim is left feeling helpless and very alone. Bullies also control onlookers, those who should help the victim but, instead, turn away. Thus, victims are hurt twice, once by the bully's physical or emotional abuse and a second time by the silent acceptance of bystanders. Because bullies control the situation, victims usually have little options for responding. Some victims fight back, which can put them at risk for injury, disciplinary action, or jail. Other victims internalize the hurt, blaming and attacking themselves. This internalization can lead to eating disorders, depression, or suicide. While investigating school attacks, the U.S. Secret Service discovered that many school attackers had a history of bullying victimization. These seasoned investigators described the bullying attacks as so severe that, if the same incidents had occurred in the workplace, the bullies would have been fired or charged with criminal offenses. Schools should be safe places for children. No one deserves to be tormented to the point where he or she feels that homicide or suicide is a way out. Bystanders, friends, and family members have an obligation to help others and, particularly, victims of abuse. Despite an apparent reluctance to get involved, there are advantages to helping victims. Helping the disadvantaged and disenfranchised in the community creates heroes. Our society needs more heroes, people who are courageous enough to step up and help those who are hurt, abused, put down, or humiliated.

In this book, bullying is presented from a medical perspective, describing symptoms of bullying, how to diagnose bullying, its causes, adverse consequences, treatment, and prevention. The goal of the book is to provide a deeper understanding of bullying so that this very basic form of violence is stopped before it destroys further lives and communities.

Chapter 1, "Bullying Is a Health Issue," deconstructs the belief that violence is a criminal justice issue. Violence causes untold injuries, deaths, and disabilities around the world. Easy access to weapons elevates the potential for violence and the severity of violence-related injuries. Across the nation, health care workers are forced to treat violence every day. One inner city emergency room in Philadelphia referred to themselves as "The Knife and Gun Club," a disdainful reference to the devastating injuries seen and treated. For a variety of reasons, youth account for more than their fair share of violence-related injuries and deaths. The economic and social cost of youth violence is astounding. Yet, violence does not escalate overnight. Violence-related behaviors increase gradually over time. Violence starts when offenders test antisocial behaviors and no one corrects the behaviors. Bullying is an early form of violence. Bullying impacts the physical, the emotional, the intellectual, the social, and the spiritual health of the victim. In addition to explaining how youth violence and bullying are medical issues, this chapter presents early research into bullying and bullying prevention. Many groundbreaking discoveries provided a solid foundation for effective and thoughtful solutions. By approaching bullying as a medical issue and knowing the science behind bullying prevention, we can effectively understand and eliminate the problem.

The first chapter provides overviews of a few of the many heartbreaking cases of suicides and homicides due to bullying. These cases captured the interest of people around the world, not because of the bullying, but because of the outcomes of bullying. In the United States, school attacks can be traced back to colonial times. Reviewing cases of school attacks, where the attacker was the victim of bullying, reveals several important themes. Panic alarms, metal detectors, and profiling school attackers are ineffective ways to stop a school attack. The best way to stop a youth attacker is when a caring, concerned adult reaches out to the potential attacker, makes a personal connection, and helps the youth to feel valued as an individual. (Note that this method is not effective for adult or narcissistic attackers.) A second theme that emerged is that, when attacks did occur, surviving attackers were usually filled with intense remorse. Many youth attackers committed suicide or begged someone to kill them after the attack. A third theme is that judges are very unsympathetic to school attackers. The offenders are usually given extremely harsh penalties. Bullying victimization does not inspire leniency. Despite the enormous media attention given to school attacks, schools are relatively safe places. Other case studies show how victims were tormented to the point of suicide. The victim was so consumed and confused by the abuse that he or she was not able to think clearly. These suicides provide valuable lessons. When the victim starts to believe that he or she deserves the abuse and that suffering can only be alleviated through death, family and friends must step in. No one deserves to be bullied and, especially, to the point where he or she can no longer think clearly. No one deserves to be driven to the point of suicide. School attacks and suicide are not effective ways to deal with the problem. These actions make the problem worse. There are other ways to deal with the pain and humiliation of bullying.

Chapter 2, "The Definition of Bullying," describes actions that constitute bullying and how these behaviors differ from other forms of violence. Bullying is an imbalance of power where the bully has greater power than the victim. The bully intentionally abuses his or her power to hurt the victim. This chapter explains the different types of power and how people can abuse power. The main lesson is that power is fluid. Power can shift from one person to another or from one group to another. Because power is fluid, it is very foolish of people to abuse their power. The old saying, "what goes around, comes around," is applicable. Understanding power and the fluidity of power can help victims and bullies. The victim can identify and draw on other sources of power to temper or stop the abuse. Those who abuse others should consider what will happen to them when power shifts from the tormenter to the tormented. They may find themselves at the mercy of their victims. The power differential extends beyond the bully–victim relationship. Bullying would not be bullying if bullies did not control henchmen and bystanders. The role of others, such as henchman, cosigner, disengaged onlooker, possible defender, and defender, are described. The chapter concludes with an overview of the different and varied methods that bullies use to hurt their victims. Understanding the dynamics between bully, victim, and bystanders provides insight into bullying and allows people to name the behavior as abuse. Naming the behavior, calling an action bullying, provides a diagnosis that determines appropriate treatment.

Chapter 3, "Prevalence," presents statistics on bullying. Knowing how common bullying is, who is impacted by bullying, and the different types of bullying that occur helps scientists to understand the extent of the problem and to compare bullying within different places and populations. In comparing different groups, scientists can identify what factors increase risk and what factors protect against victimization. High-risk groups for victimization are youth with disabilities and youth who are lesbian, gay, or bisexual. The common factor that places all of these youth at higher risk is the number and quality of friendships or social support. Youth who do not have close, supportive friends are at higher risk for victimization. How well an individual is accepted by those in the community determines susceptibility to bullying or other forms of social ostracism. This research finding provides important insights into alleviating bullying. History has demonstrated over and over again that characteristics rejected by one group may be accepted and honored by another group. The chapter concludes with the case of Ed Roberts, a quadriplegic who, statistically, should have been at very high risk of social rejection and bullying. With the love and support of those around him, Ed learned to deal with his physical differences with dignity and grace. Ed rose above what society said he should or should not have been to become a leader in the disability civil rights movement. Social support, feeling connected to friends and community, provides a protective shield against bullying.

Chapter 4, "Diagnosis," cuts through the lies, excuses, and accusations of the bully to identify who is the victim and who is the perpetrator. Knowing the symptoms of victimization and the symptoms of perpetration helps bystanders to accurately identify the victim and the bully. Accurate diagnosis directs appropriate interventions where the victim is protected, the bully is redirected, and bystanders are empowered to stop the incidents. The chapter presents some of the tricks that bullies use to set victims up for attack and to undermine victim reporting. Onlookers must be careful not to get drawn into the bully's delusional thinking. In holding firm with an accurate diagnosis, onlookers can set limits on bullying and direct the victim toward supportive resources.

Chapter 5, "Health Consequences," describes the devastating outcomes of victimization. In addition to the emotional and social effects of bullying, chronic abuse is a toxic stressor. Toxic stress changes the way that the human body breaks down and uses carbohydrates, fats, and proteins. These changes increase risk of infection, high blood pressure, heart disease, and other chronic health problems. Victims can suffer from post-traumatic stress disorder and betrayal trauma. Bullies also suffer. When bullies are allowed to bully, they are deprived of the opportunity to learn normal, acceptable social behavior. Without appropriate limits, they will continue to push social boundaries until they end up in trouble and sometimes, jail. Bullying has consequences on schools and communities. The estimated cost of bullying in a typical high school serving 1,000 students is $2.3 million per year. It is taxpayers who bear the burden. In communities where bullying has been going on for several generations, the community members, parents, grandparents, aunts, and uncles have lost trust in school authorities. Distrust may be expressed as a lack of support for the school, passive–aggressive communication, open disrespect, or anger. In communities where bullying was a chronic and unabated problem, schools must work very hard to undo past betrayals. Truth and reconciliation offer one model for helping communities to heal from the trauma of past injustices.

Chapter 6, "Causes of Bullying," starts by explaining the criteria that biomedical researchers must meet in order to say with certainty that a problem causes a particular outcome. In medicine and social sciences, it is very difficult to meet all or some of these criteria. Human beings are complex organisms. What severely impacts one person may not affect another. This chapter discusses the most common biopsychosocial factors that increase the risk of violence. Factors exist on an individual, social, and organizational level. Models and theories are presented as ways to understand the complex attitudes and behaviors. Models and theories not only explain why bullies bully, but also why victims and bystanders react in the ways that they do. Models and theories also suggest effective, scientifically based ways to deal with the problem.

Chapter 7, "Treatment and Prevention," discusses the multiple ways to intervene and prevent bullying. Intervention consists of stopping bullying when it occurs. Standing up for the victim can minimize the social isolation experienced by victims and strengthen resilience. Prevention aims to stop bullying before it begins. Prevention is achieved by building caring, concerned communities who respect and welcome all people. The ideal learning community provides equal rights and power. Each person has the right to life, liberty, and the pursuit of happiness. Each person has the right to learn. Treatment consists of helping the victim to heal from the abuse and helping the bully to deal with the normal frustrations of life in more positive ways. It may take decades for schools to rebuild lost trust and for communities to heal from the past abuses.

Section Two, "Controversies and Issues," discusses some of the current struggles in bullying prevention. People have strong ideas about bullying and other forms of youth violence. These ideas can influence reactions to bullying. Unfortunately, many cases of bullying are treated based on these personal philosophies and local politics. The purpose of this section is to deconstruct some of the current myths and misconceptions regarding bullying and to offer current and accurate information based on scientific research. Approaching youth violence from a scientific, holistic perspective can minimize the number of deaths and injuries due to violence.

Section Three, "Resources," describes recommended sources of information. Many of the best resources in youth violence prevention are available at no cost. In an effort to optimize the health and well-being of Americans, the federal government is committed to studying diseases.

State and federal governments fund research projects on the leading causes of death and disability, including research into youth violence, school violence, dating violence, suicide, and other mental health problems. Because this research is paid for by public funding, the information gained from the research is available free of charge. This section identifies some of the best sources of information available on bullying and bullying prevention. These are excellent, quality sources of information and a good place to start for anyone interested in studying bullying prevention.

Bullying severely damages physical and emotional health. It can have catastrophic effects on the victim, bystanders, the community, and the bully. Yet, bullying, itself, is not the problem. The problem is how victims and bystanders respond to bullying. If a bully tried to abuse someone and others stepped in to stop the abuse, the victim would feel empowered, cherished, and respected. The victim would not suffer from the humiliation of abuse and fear of future attacks. The victim would be secure in knowing that others could be trusted for care and support. This book aims to deconstruct some of the misleading ideas that stop bystanders from getting involved and provides constructive ways to intervene and treat the problem. Merely stopping bullying may not be enough to help the victims. Because bullying has been allowed to go on for so long in some communities, it is imperative that leaders acknowledge past injustices and make a firm commitment to work with the community to promote a positive educational experience for all children. The most effective way to teach children not to bully is for adults to model care and respect. Children learn to treat others with kindness and respect when they, themselves, have been treated with kindness and respect.

Introduction

Interpersonal disagreements are a normal part of life. Whenever people care deeply about issues in their family or community, there is a potential for disagreement. Each person sees the issue from a unique perspective and wants this perspective to be recognized. Although disagreement can be uncomfortable, it can also be beneficial. Disagreement means that people care about a topic. Caring is the first step toward doing something about a problem. Bullying *is not* a disagreement. Bullying is an abusive, malicious, and intentionally hurtful action. It is important to differentiate interpersonal disagreements from bullying because confusing the two can unintentionally harm the victim of bullying. In interpersonal disputes, people are trying to solve a common problem. As long as both parties respect each other, they should be able to work together to reach an agreeable solution. In bullying, the bully is not trying to solve a problem. The bully is trying to hurt the victim. Encouraging the victim to work with the bully will only promote further abuse. Bullies use various tactics to hurt victims, including hitting, kicking, punching, stealing, name-calling, spreading nasty rumors, or intentionally excluding the victim from a group of peers. These behaviors are not normal. Bullies don't stop at the physical, verbal, or emotional attacks. Bullies not only crush their victims, they kick them while they are down. Bullies manipulate friends, family members, and loved ones to isolate and hurt the victim. Bullying is not a disagreement or interpersonal dispute. Bullying is a type of interpersonal violence. Recognizing bullying as a type of abuse provides a deeper understanding of the problem and insights into addressing the issue. Mediators must use different techniques for bullying than are used for interpersonal disagreements.

Victims of bullying suffer from severe emotional pain. Bullying is associated with increased drug use, eating disorders, and depression. The most notable and horrific outcomes of bullying are suicides and homicides. How the victim responds depends on the victim's personality, past experiences, ways of dealing with stress, and how much the victim cares about the situation. Most targets of bullying are left stunned. They do not understand what they did to deserve such harsh treatment. The overly aggressive, exaggerated attacks by the bully compounded with apparent acceptance by would-be friends, peers, and strangers is soul-destroying. Some victims respond with counter attack, fighting back with fists, words, or allies. A few victims turn to gun violence, lashing out at the bully, henchmen, bystanders, and others in the community who allowed the abuse. Other victims retreat into themselves, secretly and silently submitting to the bully's torture. Too many young people have died over bullying. This book seeks to show other responses to bullying that will help the victim move away from the bully, to heal from the trauma, and to live a successful, happy life.

In order to move forward, past attitudes and reactions to bullying must be revised. Bullying is no longer considered a rite of passage. Bullying is no longer considered an act that builds character. Bullying is a social issue that hurts victims, the bullies, bystanders, family members, schools, and communities. In an effort to deter school attacks and suicides due to bullying, school officials initially turned to whatever was available. Schools installed multimillion dollar panic alarm systems and metal detectors, mandated see-through book bags, and invited guest speakers to talk to students. Unfortunately, these ideas were merely a Band-Aid. They helped adults to feel better. They didn't actually solve the problem. Bullies continued to bully. Children continued to die. Schools have come a long way since the early, uninformed days of bullying prevention. Research studies have identified many successful anti-bullying and anti-violence strategies. Bullying can be treated while it is occurring and can be prevented before it occurs. New programs based on the science of how children learn and think promise the most effective solutions to the problem.

Effective bullying prevention starts with caring, concerned adults who promote dignity and respect for all people in the school community. Although these concepts may sound simple and idyllic, in reality, they are very difficult to achieve. Building caring, inclusive, and welcoming communities is a challenge. Americans value independence, competition, and power. These values are more characteristic of the bully than the victim. Thus, bully-like traits are honored in American society. To compound the problem, violence, watching a person get hurt, is entertainment. Children's exposure to violence in the home, community, and media promotes widespread acceptance of violence. In order for schools to develop caring, concerned learning communities, they must first deconstruct social values that promote violence. Some people might argue that it is not the responsibility of schools to teach social values. It is the right and responsibility of parents and family members to determine how children should relate to their peers and environment. In unsafe communities, teaching children to care for others may make the child vulnerable to abuse. In dangerous neighborhoods, children must appear tough and independent in order to survive. To some degree, these beliefs are true. In communities where children must be street-smart, teaching children nonviolent techniques may make them appear more vulnerable. Welcoming strangers into a friendship too quickly can set the person up for abuse. In communities where people are wary and cautious, children can be taught to code switch. Code switching refers to when a person acts one way in one situation and another way in a different situation. For example, walking through a dark alley at night requires that a person walk with confidence, toughness, or a hard facial grimace. The same demeanor is not necessary when walking into a church, synagogue, or mosque. Children know to act differently in different situations. Teaching children to code switch and to act with care and compassion at school can promote positive learning environments. When adults also interact respectfully, show compassion for others, and build positive, supportive relationships, children learn not to bully.

True bullying prevention occurs when *everyone* in the community is treated with dignity and respect. Respect does not simply mean putting out a welcome mat for those who are different. Respect means acknowledging the social injustices that exist in many communities, supporting people who are discriminated against, and honoring children as children. True bullies are leaders in the communities. Bullies have money, stature, and power. True bullies are the star athletes, the popular girls, the son or daughter of school or township officials. Bullies feel entitled to abuse others because they have never been taught how to respect others. They do not know how to use their power appropriately. In order to stop bullying, schools must stand up to the wealthy and powerful families in the community. Schools can no longer passively accept bullying by children with social connections. And in communities where bullying has occurred repeatedly for multiple generations, schools have to build trust. The community cannot establish a caring, bully-free environment until past scars have been healed. Grandparents, parents, and aunts, and uncles who suffered from bullying must be helped to heal. Healing can be achieved by acknowledging past wrongs and injustices and making a firm commitment to protect future generations from abuse. Comprehensive bullying prevention requires a careful balance between setting limits and recognizing children's need to test different behaviors. In an attempt to stop bullying, many schools picked up the zero tolerance mantra. In theory, zero tolerance is good. It means that schools do not tolerate any bullying. In reality, zero tolerance is a myth. School officials often look the other way when the bully is the school disciplinarian, a tenured teacher, the school board president, or the school board president's son. These individuals are not thrown out, ejected from schools, yet youth without social power meet harsh, punitive consequences when they bully. There needs to be a common ground where bullying is recognized as bullying and the offender is kindly reminded not to bully others. True tolerance means accepting all people, including those who bully. Teaching children to be kind to each other, monitoring behaviors, and respectfully correcting bullying as it occurs is more effective than zero tolerance. People who abuse others should be encouraged (not forced, berated, or belittled) to reflect on how they interact with other people and how they would want others to interact with them.

Sections One and Two of this book present bullying from a biopsychosocial perspective, from a medical perspective. The biological and psychological perspectives explain why people hurt other people, why victims respond in the ways that they do, and how these processes impact the body. The sociological perspective explains how people can learn to interact in positive ways and to build positive relationships and collaborative communities. The biopsychosocial perspective provides insights, ideas, theories, and suggestions to stop abusive relationships and to help victims heal. Alleviating bullying requires a complex, multifaceted approach that is based on a scientific understanding of social systems and effective mental health treatments. Solutions must include the offenders, the victims, the bystanders, and the community. True bullying prevention is achieved when people recognize the existing power imbalances in society and are willing to give up power. Surprisingly, people actually gain power when they give up power. Shared power provides healthy communities where all individuals may grow and flourish.

SECTION I

CHAPTER 1

Bullying is a Health Issue

Injuries are the leading cause of death of people between the ages of 1 and 44 in the United States. Violence is one of the main causes of injuries. Violence accounts for 51,000 deaths per year and more than half a million emergency room visits. Examples of violence-related deaths and injuries are gunshot wounds, human bites, amputations, cuts, or broken bones. Beyond those seeking treatment in hospitals, a lot more people are treated in doctors' offices, clinics, or at home.

The highest risk group for death and injury due to violence is young people. Homicide, the second leading cause of youth death, accounts for 5,700 deaths per year. Suicide ranks third, with 4,400 youth deaths per year (CDC, 2010). The annual cost of medical care and lost productivity for all violence-related injuries exceeds $47 billion. The effects reach far beyond the victims; violence traumatizes family members, friends, and bystanders. In an effort to stop the unnecessary suffering of violence, doctors, nurses, public health workers, counselors and other medical practitioners, and researchers have identified treatments that are most effective in preventing violence. Preventing violence-related deaths and injuries often starts with preventing bullying, a form of violence that is endemic in many schools and communities. The careful application of evidence-based treatments, those treatments that have been proven effective in stopping bullying, can reduce the exacerbation of bullying into violence and therefore prevent the pain and trauma of violence-related deaths and injuries.

There are many different types of violence. Dating violence, road rage, bullying, self-mutilation (cutting or burning), weapon carrying, and media violence are just a few forms of violence. Bullying is a specific type of violence that occurs among people of all ages and in many diverse communities. Bullying occurs in homes, schools, communities, and workplaces throughout the United States, Canada, Great Britain, Japan, and in other countries around the world. Bullying occurs among wealthy, middle class, and poor communities. Both males and females perpetrate and are victims of bullying. Bullying is very common and exists within many social groups. In the United States, an estimated 1.6 million school students are bullied at least once a week and 1.7 million youth bully others (U.S. Department of Justice, 2001).

Bullying was once believed to be an irritating, but relatively harmless, behavior. Some adults even believed that bullying made a child tougher, more able to deal with other people in life. We now know that these philosophies were wrong. Bullying causes multiple health problems for the victims, the bystanders, and the bullies themselves. Victims suffer from cuts, bruises, anxiety, depression, inability to trust others, suicidal ideation, and psychosomatic complaints, such as headaches or stomachaches.

Some victims turn to violence as a way to fight back against the bullying. This counter-aggression puts victims at risk of further injury, disciplinary action, or criminal charges. Bystanders of bullying are also affected. They report very high levels of stress. On a scale measuring stress levels, bystanders score at about the same level as people experiencing severely life-threatening events, such as floods or fires. Bullies, themselves, suffer because they do not learn normal social behaviors. Bullies will continue to push the limits and are at higher risk of incarceration as other young adults.

At the community level, bullying interferes with normal child development. In schools, bullying interferes with learning. In an environment ripe with bullying, students become focused on the bullying and are distracted from learning. The inability to learn produces long-term disparities in earning potential, which will impact later health and well-being. Beyond the direct health consequences of bullying, bullying often coexists with other health problems, such as attention deficit hyperactivity disorder (ADHD), drug abuse, depression, or psychiatric disorders. Bullying is an extremely complex problem. Studying bullying from a health perspective can lead to effective solutions.

Bullying is unusual in that it qualifies as an unhealthy behavior, a symptom, and a disease, all at the same time. The hitting, pushing, kicking, name-calling, rumors, and social exclusion of bullying are all unhealthy behaviors. Physical bullying increases risk of injury for both the perpetrator and the victim. Verbal and emotional bullying causes emotional stress, which can impact mental health. Name calling, excluding, and spreading nasty rumors can cause depression, eating disorders, thoughts of suicide or homicide, all of which are alarming health issues.

Bullying is also a symptom in that it serves as a warning sign of an unhealthy school or workplace. Conflicts occur whenever people are passionate and engaged in issues. A healthy, peaceful community is not without conflict. The difference between a peaceful community and an unhealthy community is that peaceful communities use civilized methods to resolve conflicts. Each member of the group understands the purpose of the group and works together to achieve a common goal. Disagreements and competition are handled in ways that respect and benefit all members of the group. In unhealthy communities, conflict and competition are handled through coercion or bullying. As new members enter the group, they also learn to bully, and bullying becomes a way of life. When a disease is deeply interwoven into the community, it becomes endemic. The problem with endemic bullying is that the members of the community become focused on the bullying and are distracted from the group's original missions or goals. Group members waste time in either scheming to bully or avoiding, denying, or covering up the bullying. These maneuvers steal time away from the true group function and produce a highly dysfunctional, nonproductive school or workplace. Whereas the function of healthy societies is to work together to achieve an intended outcome, the group that suffers from bullying tends to focus on the bullying and not what they are supposed to focus on. Ultimately, the distraction caused by bullying can mean the downfall of an organization.

Because bullying has only recently become recognized as a health issue in the United States, there is still much research and education to be done in the field. Scientists have identified who are at high risk for bullying, victimization, and perpetration, where bullying occurs, and programs to prevent bullying. Neurologists have identified changes in the brain that occur when children are exposed to chronic violence—changes that impact the rest of the child's life. The next steps are to deconstruct some of the myths about bullying, study effective treatments, and promote programs that work in schools and communities. There is still much work to be done in the field of violence research and prevention. Students interested in the field of violence prevention are encouraged to contact violence prevention researchers and experts to find out more about the field.

The Definition of Health

The World Health Organization defines health as "a state of complete physical, mental and social well-being, and not merely the absence of disease" (Preamble to the Constitution of the World Health Organization as adopted by the International Health Conference, New York, June 19–July 22, 1946; Official Records of the World Health Organization, no. 2, p. 100). This definition of health has not changed since 1946, an indication that the original authors very accurately expressed health as a holistic concept with multiple dimensions. The specific dimensions of health—physical, emotional, intellectual, social, and spiritual—are all impacted by bullying.

Physical health is the dimension that describes how the body functions on a day-to-day basis, including how the body responds to illness or injury. It is easy to see how hitting, kicking, or pushing someone—physical forms of bullying—can cause lacerations, bruising, or scars. It is more difficult to see how psychological bullying, such as relational exclusion or name-calling, affects physical health. Yet, it does. When the victims or bystanders experience stress, their bodies respond with a biochemical cascade. The biochemical reactions give the person a temporary boost of energy to enable a rapid response. This temporary boost provides energy and oxygen that allow the person to fight or run away from the threat. Unfortunately, the response is achieved by stealing resources from other areas of the body. For example, the body produces glucose to provide a quick fuel for muscles. The glucose is manufactured by breaking down proteins in the body. Some of these proteins would normally fight infections or build muscle. Without these proteins, the body is susceptible to viral or bacterial attack, and the body muscles deteriorate. During times of stress, the heart works harder to send oxygen to the muscles. This means an increase in blood pressure, which can cause heart disease, kidney disease, or stroke in at-risk individuals. Thus, the stress of name-calling, social exclusion, or false rumors may adversely affect physical health.

Emotional health is the feeling that a person has about self, other people, circumstances, or environment. Bullying makes a person feel bad about himself, peers, and school. Persistent bullying causes depression, self-hatred, anger, and distrust in other relationships. Victims carry the weight of sadness into everything that they do.

Intellectual health refers to how people acquire, filter, and use health information. People with high intellectual health gather information from reputable and trustworthy sources, discern whether the information is accurate and honest, filter the information, discarding poor quality information, and carefully weigh the advantages and disadvantages of recommendations before taking action. With bullying, the victim is often in a state of stress and not thinking clearly. They are highly vulnerable to misguided thinking about how to handle the situation or pervasive thoughts supporting self-destructive behaviors.

Social health refers to the ability of a person to feel comfortable and enjoy the companionship of other people. Bullies function by manipulating the social group, by damaging the victim's reputation or status. It is often the social damage that hurts victims more than physical or verbal attack. When friends and classmates do not stand up for the victim during an attack, they add to the victim's pain. The lack of intervention can push victims into feeling unimportant and worthless to friends, family members, and other members of the community. Social health, the ability to feel comfortable and enjoy the companionship of surrounding people, is threatened by the bully's actions and by the bystanders' reactions.

The last component of health, *spirituality,* is the feeling that a person's life is in harmony with thoughts, actions, and surroundings. Spirituality can be an appreciation for a higher being, nature, art, literature, or other human beings and is evidenced by an outward expression of that appreciation. Many ancient cultures believed in the interconnectedness of man and nature. Spiritual health is balanced when lifestyle, behavior, and values are consistent with each other. For example, if a person values nature and is able to take walks in the woods, visit a beach, or sit in a park, the person may feel connected to the world and others. In bullying, the victims' spiritual health suffers because they may find it difficult to enjoy their favorite activities. Fears of safety or humiliation invade the victim's thoughts. Bystanders are also impacted. When core values—a respect for peace and justice—are inconsistent with real life—watching another person being bullied—spiritual health is impacted. Understanding the full impact of bullying on every aspect of health provides a deeper understanding of the problem and insights into helping victims.

Optimal health is not the achievement of excellence in all of these categories. It would be very difficult to achieve the perfect physical, emotional, intellectual, social, and spiritual health, and this would mean that people with disease or disabilities, such as epilepsy, ADHD, dyslexia, or heart disease, could never be healthy. Health is a balance of all these components. Thus, when someone is being hurt, socially through bullying, an equal and positive counterbalance to the hurt can bring the victim back into a healthy state. The counterbalance can be achieved through the same component as that which is being impacted by the bullying. For example, a counterbalance to the social isolation of bullying at school is to find social interactions in other places in the community, such as sports teams, clubs, or houses of worship. A counterbalance can also be achieved through a different component, such as engaging in yoga, taking a walk, painting, or singing a song—examples of different types of spiritual exercises. If bullying is the disease, victims who are actively living with bullying can and must find other ways to balance their physical, mental, and social well-being in order that they may heal despite the bullying.

How Researchers Study Bullying

There are many different ways to study bullying. The most commonly used methods are surveys and public records. Surveys and public records provide general statistics on the number of people impacted by bullying, where bullying occurs, characteristics of bullies and victims, and attitudes toward bullying. These data are important because they help people who work with youth to understand who is at risk for bullying, victimization, and perpetration and the best ways to help those at risk. Government organizations, such as the Centers for Disease Control and Prevention, state and local health departments, or Department of Justice, summarize and report large volumes of data that would normally be very difficult for one individual to retrieve and analyze. For example, the Centers for Disease Control and Prevention provide data on the total number of violence-related deaths or injuries. Other sources of public records are schools, hospitals, and health departments. Schools gather and report data on serious incidents, suspensions, and expulsions. Some states now require schools to report and count the number of bullying incidents. Hospitals can provide data on the number of emergency room visits due to violence and the average cost of violence-related incidents. These forms of data, also known as preexisting data, are convenient but do not give much detail on why or how incidents occurred.

Field studies are a type of study that involves observing people in a natural setting to provide a contextual understanding of the problem. Researchers originally observed children at play and in school to learn more about bullying. Case studies are specific types of field study that provide detailed accounts of one person's or a small group of people's lives. Case studies help the researcher to understand bully–victim–bystander interactions leading up to bullying, reactions of victims that may stall, stop, or exacerbate further bullying, and the short- and long-term effects on the victim, the bully, and the bystanders. Case studies have an advantage over surveys and existing data in that case studies are able to describe and discern subtle behaviors and complex interactions that may not be noticeable through other methods. Case studies have been extremely important in bullying research. Cases such as the Columbine High School shooting, Phoebe Prince, Megan Meier, and Tyler Clementi helped people to understand the implications of bullying and to support bullying research and prevention in schools and communities. A limitation of case studies is that they report a very unique group of interactions that lead to specific outcomes. Just because one outcome occurs with one case study or individual does not mean that the same outcome will occur for all people. For example, it is believed that the youth who attacked Columbine were originally the victims of bullying by athletes in Columbine High School. It would be faulty logic to assume that every youth bullied by a school athlete will attack his or her school. While case studies provide insights, just how far the insights will apply to other people is debatable.

Laboratory studies are a type of study that test how people respond to a specific stimulus, such as viewing a violent movie or video game. Laboratory studies have an experimental group, the group that receives the stimulus, and a control group, the group that receives no stimulus or receives a neutral stimulus. Laboratory studies compare the groups at the beginning and end of the experiment to identify differences. A limitation of laboratory studies is that they are often performed in a controlled environment where outside, moderating factors are removed. Eliminating moderating factors is not a realistic reflection of what happens in the real world. In the real world, friends, classmates, teachers, and other adults can influence how a child acts. Laboratory studies may not capture these outside influences and can lead to faulty conclusions.

Intervention studies may be a combination of surveys, existing data, case studies, or laboratory studies without the moderating variables removed. Intervention studies test a specific intervention, such as a school policy against bullying or a bullying prevention program, to determine what works and what does not work to reduce bullying. Intervention studies can use data from a variety of different sources, such as surveys, preexisting data, and case studies. Studying bullying through different methods and sources of data is ideal because each data source provides a unique perspective. When the different perspectives are combined, the outcome is a more comprehensive view of the problem.

The History of Bullying Research

In the 1950s, Konrad Lorenz (1966) introduced the term "mobbing" based on his lifetime of observations of animal behavior. Lorenz was born in Vienna, Austria, in 1903. As a child, he loved animals. His interest was nurtured by a nanny who read books about animals to him and encouraged him to raise salamanders. *Nils Holgersson* by Selma Lagerlof was a popular book at the time. Nils was a fictitious character, a young boy who traveled through Sweden with wild geese. After hearing the story, Lorenz wanted to be a wild goose. He quickly realized that it was not possible for a boy to turn into a goose and, instead, set his sights on owning domesticated ducks. A neighbor gave Lorenz a one-day-old duckling. The duckling quickly bonded with his young keeper, who was intrigued by the duck's behavior. Lorenz noted the differences and similarities between his duck and other wild water fowl. Lorenz's interest in birds continued through elementary school, where he learned about primitive birds and read books on evolution. By the end of high school, Lorenz wanted to study paleontology or zoology. His father wanted him to become a doctor. Lorenz yielded to his father's wishes and attended medical school. In medical school, anatomy classes provided further opportunities to study evolution. Lorenz embraced anatomy and physiology because it allowed him to make comparisons between humans and other species. In 1941, Lorenz joined the German army, where he worked as a neurologist and psychologist. In 1942, he was captured by the Russians. He continued

Konrad Lorenz identified the concept of mobbing (the original term for bullying) based on his observations of ducks and geese. When Lorenz saw a gaggle of geese attack a fox, he realized that animals act differently in a group. The idea of herd behavior provides insights into why henchmen and bystanders go along with bullying. (Sara Ann Kuykendall)

working as a prisoner of war/doctor in hospitals and small camps. During his imprisonment, he started writing. However, his topics were limited. He could not write about his favorite topic—human behavior—because it may have been misinterpreted as political incitement. Instead, he wrote about the study of knowledge.

On returning from the war, Lorenz resumed his study of water fowl. His early interests in avian behavior, experiences in Nazi Germany, and time as a prisoner of war allowed him to make connections between aggressive behavior in animals and aggressive behavior in humans. Lorenz developed the concept of mobbing after watching a gaggle of geese attack a fox. Lorenz defined mobbing as a group of animals joining together to attack a stronger predator. The idea of mobbing opened the door to the study of herd behavior, the idea that animals in a group will act differently than one animal acting alone. Herding is believed to provide protection to individual members of the group. This protection is achieved through several different mechanisms. It is harder for a predator to pick out any one target within a group because the group serves as a distraction. Typically, a predator studies the strengths and weaknesses of a prey, thereby planning an attack that will minimize the prey's strengths and maximize its weaknesses. When the predator is distracted by other members of the herd, the attack is weakened. The predator may make mistakes that would not have been made if the predator were paying full attention.

Herding also distributes the attack across more potential targets. An individual alone or in a group of two has a 50 percent risk of attack, five times higher than an individual in a group of ten, where the risk of attack is 10 percent. It is also harder for the predator to pluck one target from the group, and this lessens the severity of the attack.

Because Lorenz was able to compare domestic animals with wild animals, Lorenz concluded that mobbing was inherent in both wild and domesticated animals. He concluded that some behaviors are passed down from generation to generation and these behaviors probably aid in survival. The herd can act as an aggressor or a protector, depending on the animal, the circumstances, and the herd. Lorenz wrote several books, focusing on animal psychology, and was one of three people awarded the 1973 Nobel Prize in Physiology for observations of individual and social behavior.

In the 1960s, Dr. Albert Bandura, a Canadian American psychologist, conducted a series of laboratory studies to investigate what causes people to act violently. In these experiments, children were exposed to an adult who modeled either aggressive or nonaggressive behavior during play. Seventy-two children were divided into three groups: a control group, a group exposed to aggressive behavior, and another group exposed to nonaggressive play. The group exposed to nonaggressive behavior was further divided into children exposed to an adult of the same gender (a male child exposed to a male adult or a female child exposed to a female adult) or a different gender model (a male child exposed to a female model and a female child exposed to a male model). The aggressive play group was also subdivided into same child–adult gender and different child–adult gender groups. The adult models followed a script where they started with nonaggressive play and, then, after a minute, punched or attacked a Bobo Doll—a tall, inflatable clown. The researcher then entered the room, excused the adult, and took the child into a second room. The second room contained better toys. The purpose of the second room was to frustrate the child because, after a very short period of time, the researcher would take the child back to the original room.

Bandura's research team found that the children who observed the aggressive adult were 16–17 times more likely to show aggression than children exposed to the nonaggressive adult. Males exhibited more aggressive behavior than females and those children who observed aggressive modeling by an adult of the same gender acted more aggressively than children who observed an aggressive adult of the opposite gender. Bandura also noted that the children did not merely imitate the aggressive behavior.

They created their own styles and forms of attack, which went beyond those that were modeled.

Based on the Bobo Doll experiments and subsequent studies, Bandura developed a theory of how people learn (Bandura, 1977). The theory provides a partial explanation of why some children are aggressive. As with any laboratory experiment, it does not account for all aggressive behaviors. The theory, known as Social Cognitive Theory, continues to develop and evolve as researchers learn more about how people take in and store information.

At the age of seven, Peter Paul Heinemann's family fled Germany to escape Jewish persecution. The family moved to Sweden, where Heinemann studied to become a doctor. Using his medical expertise to answer listener's questions, Heinemann became a popular radio talk show host. Because of his experiences as a child and a caregiver, Heinemann was extremely interested in how stereotypes and racial prejudices harm people. At the same time, the civil rights movement of the 1960s was increasing public concern about social and political policies that favored specific groups while causing disadvantage to others. Heinemann's talk show went beyond discussions of diseases to include such current issues as apartheid, drug abuse, and violence. In his presentations, Heinemann recalled an incident from 1969, when he saw a group of children attacking another child in a schoolyard. The victim ran past Heinemann, losing a shoe in the escape. Heinemann was struck by how helpless, desperate, and fearful the victim must have been. In describing this case to others, Heinemann used the term mobbing. The term caught on and was subsequently applied to group attacks.

In 1983, three Norwegian youths committed suicide as a result of peer abuse. The Norwegian public was horrified and called for action. Norwegians viewed the problem as a social problem and having to do with society at large, not as an individual problem, disconnected from the rest of society. The Norwegian Ministry of Education and Research recruited researchers from the University of Bergen to study the problem and to propose workable solutions. The researchers substituted the term bullying for mobbing because they wanted to break away from the association with Nazi Germany. The researchers adopted the term from a genre of books describing the life of students in British boarding schools. The word bully-boy described mean boys who were cruel to younger and weaker children. *Tom Brown's Schooldays* by Thomas Hughes (1857) describes a young boy's horrific experiences with a bully at Rugby School in England, a school the author attended from 1834–1842. *Harry Potter* is a later version of this genre, with Draco Malfoy's character as the bully. Although the researchers were attempting to break away from the German association, the word bully actually developed from the word *boele*, meaning sweetheart or lover in West Germanic dialects (http://www.merriam-webster.com/dictionary/bully). The word gradually developed into a term to describe a man who solicited business for prostitutes, otherwise known as a pimp. Characteristically, pimps viewed the prostitutes as personal property and protected the prostitute from attacks by clients or deranged individuals who saw prostitutes as easy targets. This protection usually came at a price, meaning that the *boele*, himself, abused the prostitute. Thus, the term eventually developed from a positive meaning to a derogatory meaning, referring nowadays to a person who abused people who are weaker or unable to protect themselves. The word bully can be used as both a noun and a verb. Bully describes either the person who commits the offense or the offense, itself.

One of the questions that the University of Bergen researchers faced was why people bullied others. Herd behavior suggests that members of the herd protect one another. It seems counter-intuitive for one human being to hurt another one. Dr. Daniel Olweus, one of the Bergen researchers, had been investigating the role of the hormones testosterone and adrenaline, and parenting as possible causes of aggression. Olweus found that while testosterone did not directly cause antisocial behavior, it did so indirectly. High testosterone levels were related to greater frustration–aggression and frustration–aggression was related to antisocial behaviors, such as bullying. The relationship between adrenaline, a hormone that is secreted during stress, and aggression was also not straightforward. Olweus found that aggression was unpleasant to young males with high adrenaline levels. These youth tried to avoid violence, while young males with low cortisol levels followed two different paths. Young males with low cortisol levels and low exposure to violence were nonaggressive and friendly and only became aggressive when provoked. Young males with low levels of cortisol and a history of exposure to violence were aggressive without provocation. Furthermore, the aggression appeared to excite the youth and prompt other risky behaviors. Olweus's studies were important because they formed the groundwork for later studies by other researchers.

In their studies of bullying, Olweus and colleagues from the University of Bergen attempted to determine who the most likely bullying victims and perpetrators are, where incidents occur, how bystanders react to bullying, and ways to prevent bullying. The early work has been replicated with other communities throughout the world, leading to a common definition of bullying. Despite differences between cultures, there are many similarities. Early beliefs that victims were selected based on unusual physical attributes, that is, red hair, freckles, or glasses, were found to be incorrect. Physical attributes of victims do not vary greatly from nonvictims. The main factor in determining who might be a victim is the number and degree of social connections. Friends are a primary factor in bullying incidents as youth who are not well connected are at higher risk of victimization. Olweus developed a model to show the common roles that people fulfill during bullying incidents. These insights were used to develop prevention strategies and to develop The Bullying Prevention Program (BPP).

The BPP was the first and only research-based program to counteract bullying in schools. The goal of the BPP was to decrease bullying by changing school norms that support bullying. The original program developers believed that schools unintentionally supported bullying by treating some students differently from others. Adults in the school may overlook bad behavior in certain students in an effort to gain favor with the parents or local politicians. For example, the son of a school board member, a star athlete, or the daughter of a wealthy family may all be treated favorably. It is easy for these children to become entitled. Since they are not held to the same standards as other students, they do not learn normal social behavior. Some students may abuse this power by bullying others. To complicate the problem, if others, from the non elite population, fight back or attempt to bully others, they are punished according to school rules. This series of events sets the precedent for injustices, where some students are allowed to bully and others are not. The BPP attempts to raise awareness of bullying as an injustice and to train school personnel to apply rules and regulations fairly. The BPP attempts to promote respect. It is not a punitive program. The intention of the program is to treat all children with respect, regardless of social power. Early studies of the program showed that the program decreased bullying by up to 50 percent (Olweus, 1993). Later evaluations showed less of an impact, with reductions of 21–38 percent (Olweus, 2003). The program authors believed that the later intervention studies may have been influenced by moderating factors. At the time of the second intervention studies, schools were focused on improving test scores. This focus may have diverted attention away from the program or may have put more stress on teachers and students, thereby causing higher levels of aggressive behaviors. Currently, the BPP is one of the few evidence-based programs to combat bullying in use in schools and Olweus is widely regarded as the grandfather of bullying prevention. The program was introduced in the United States with the help of Dr. Susan Limber of Clemson University. Dr. Limber's interest in bullying began as a young child. Limber recalled watching bullies pick on a victim at the bus stop. The behaviors disturbed her so much that she felt sick to her stomach. She wanted to do something but did not know what to do. Her interest in bullying was first formalized as an undergraduate student in college, when Limber took a random class to fill her schedule. The class on law and psychology ignited an interest in public policies protecting children.

Limber changed her major from pre-medical studies to psychology, where she studied child development and child maltreatment. Her background in child maltreatment, combined with a love of research, directed her toward the use of evidence-based programs in bullying prevention. Limber facilitated the introduction of the Olweus BPP in the United States and is a leader in public policy development regarding bullying in schools.

There is still much work to be done in bullying research and new methods of research are continually developing. Technological advances have greatly aided research. The Internet allows researchers to gather and transmit data faster than before. Social networking sites allow researchers to track and follow research participants over their entire lifetime, informing us about life trajectories for violence. Google images allow researchers to evaluate neighborhood characteristics from thousands of miles away. Advancements in biochemistry and neurology allow researchers to study the body's reaction to stress. Genetic technology allows researchers to identify genetic markers that predict a person's reaction to provocation. There is so much to learn about the causes of violence, symptoms, and treatments of bullying in society. Each study takes society one step closer toward understanding the problem and creating workable solutions.

Major Historical Events and Bullying

Most people are upset by violence and particularly upset by violence against children. In most societies, children are considered the most vulnerable population and, therefore, in need of the greatest protection. When a child is injured or dies prematurely, the entire community grieves. Even strangers feel a loss and the need to support the child's family and friends. It is because of this innate desire to protect children that school attacks impact people very strongly. People expect places where children live, play, and work to be safe. School attacks are not new. There have been more than 110 school shootings reported in the media since the 1960s. What has changed today is that advancements in communication technology allow the news of a school attack to travel to a wider audience and to spread more rapidly within a short span of time. Initially, public reactions to the news of a school attack tended to be, "It could never happen here." These incidents were considered isolated and unusual. Yet, the public's interest in keeping children safe forced journalists to dig deeper into causes of school attacks. The majority of school attacks are not due to bullying. School attacks are due to multiple factors, such as recklessness with guns, gang violence, dating violence, racism, or the paranoid thinking of mental illness. As more school attacks occurred, people started to see a connection between bullying victimization and school attacks. Interest in bullying increased and, as interest increased, parents and loved ones who lost children to suicide started to speak out about the connection between suicide and bullying. There have been several cases of school shootings and suicides due to bullying. The following sections describe just a few of the many cases.

School Attacks and Bullying

It is important to note that schools are relatively safe places. Less than 1 percent of youth homicides occur at school. The first recorded school attack in U.S. history was the Enoch Brown School Massacre that occurred on July 26, 1764, in Cumberland Valley, PA. The attack occurred during an era when European settlers were taking over land previously used and inhabited by Native Americans. Chief Pontiac, leader of the Ottawa tribe, organized warriors from different tribes to stop the encroachment. Both sides—the colonists and the Native Americans—committed murderous attacks. The attacks commonly occurred during the day, when women and children were most vulnerable because the men were out hunting or farming. On the day of the massacre, three young Lenape warriors attacked a schoolhouse. The teacher, Enoch Brown, begged for his students' lives. He tried to offer his own life in exchange for the children's freedom. His pleas were to no avail. Two of the warriors stood guard at the door as the third man attacked Brown with a tomahawk, killing and scalping him. After Brown, the warrior proceeded to scalp the 10 children present in the classroom that day. One child survived the attack. He suffered lifelong emotional problems. The warriors were severely reprimanded when they returned to the tribe. The senior members of the tribe were very upset because, even during the time of war, the young men had violated social values protecting children. Historically, the Enoch Brown Massacre is classified as the result of war. However, it is arguable that the Native Americans felt persecuted and bullied, deprived of their native land, by stronger and more powerful forces. Thus, the Enoch Brown massacre may have been the first bullying-related school attack in U.S. history.

On May 18, 1927, Andrew Kehoe, a Michigan farmer and school board member, carried out one of the bloodiest school attacks in American history. Kehoe suffered from financial problems. He was not a successful farmer; his wife had tuberculosis and her treatment strained their budget; and the school board was planning on increasing taxes. Kehoe was considered an oddball among the community. He did not use traditional farming methods. He liked to buy expensive farm equipment and spent a great deal of time tinkering with machines rather than farming. If he did use the machines, he used them incorrectly. The bank that loaned him money to buy the farm was going to take the farm away. Kehoe felt helpless against the demands for higher taxes. Instead of seeking financial guidance, Kehoe got angry, and blamed his financial problems on the school board. On the day of the attack, Kehoe killed his wife, set fire to his farm buildings, and detonated two explosions. The first explosion was at Bath Consolidated School and the second was at the rescue scene, injuring survivors and rescue workers. Kehoe killed himself in the second explosion, a suicide car bomb. 45 people died and 58 were injured; many of the deaths and injuries were young children. The attack was brutal and calculating. Kehoe probably felt bullied by the school board and powerless to deal with the situation, just like many victims of bullying. Sadly, if Kehoe had looked beyond his anger and hurt, he might have realized that the solution to his financial problems was in his own backyard. Investigators estimated that if Kehoe had sold his farm equipment, he could have paid off his entire mortgage loan.

Brenda Ann Spencer was one of the first more recent school attackers, and one of the few female attackers. Her case inspired the song, "I don't like Mondays," by British punk rock group, *The Boomtown Rats*. Spencer's parents were divorced. She lived with her father in San Diego, California. By the age of 16, Brenda was a social outcast with a troubled history of drug use, vandalism, theft, and animal abuse. Although there seemed to be no precipitating events that led up to the attack on January 29, 1979, Spencer did not appear to have a good relationship with either parent or any other involved adult. On the day of the attack, Spencer comfortably positioned herself at the living room window of her father's home with a rifle that her father had given her for Christmas. Spencer carried out a sniper-like attack on both adults and children as they entered Cleveland Elementary School. Spencer killed two people and injured nine others. After a seven-hour standoff, she surrendered to the police. When asked about her motive for the attack, Spencer responded, "I just did it for the fun of it. I don't like Mondays." Spencer was tried as an adult and sentenced to 25 years in prison for the attack. Bullying was never raised as an issue in the attack, possibly because the incident occurred before the link between bullying victimization and school attacks was highlighted. Spencer may have been the victim of a different type of violence. As Spencer became eligible for parole and was again asked why she committed the violence, Brenda alleged physical and sexual abuse by her father. The prosecutor dismissed the accusation on the grounds that Brenda had never reported the abuse before, even though it is not unusual for people of sexual abuse to repress memories of the abuse. It is only after victims are removed from the situation that they may be able to view and talk about their experiences more objectively.

School attacks are usually due to multiple factors. A review of past cases helps identify some of those factors:

- On November 15, 1995, James Ellison Rouse (17) took a rifle to Richland School in Lynnville, Tennessee, and shot two teachers and one student. One of the victims survived. Rouse later reported that violent movies and music distorted his mind, making him angry and vindictive. Rouse did not feel that he was in control of his thoughts. Rouse was tried as an adult and sentenced to life in prison without parole.
- Michael Slobodian (16) of Brampton Centennial Secondary School in Ontario, Canada, hated his English teacher, Ms. Wright. Ms. Wright would read Slobodian's papers out loud to the class and ridicule his work. On May 28, 1975, Michael tried to skip English class. Ms. Wright telephoned his mother to report him truant. Michael returned to school with two guns. He was in the men's room, preparing to attack Ms. Wright and her classroom, when a student walked in and surprised him. Slobodian shot and killed the student and went to his English classroom, where he killed Ms. Wright. Slobodian wounded 13 students before committing suicide.
- Nicholas Elliott (16) was tired of being taunted over his skin color. Elliott opened fire on teachers and students in portable classrooms at Atlantic Shores Christian School, Virginia Beach, VA, on December 16, 1988. When his gun jammed, a teacher tackled him, thwarting the attack. Elliott received a sentence of life in prison plus 114 years for causing one homicide and two injuries.
- Gary Scott Pennington (17) was from a poor family. His mother was a homemaker. His father was disabled. Despite the economic disadvantage, Scott excelled in school. His academic success attracted ire from bullies. Pennington was teased for stuttering, called names, and physically attacked. On January 18, 1993, Scott entered his English classroom with a gun, killed his English teacher and the school custodian, and then held his classmates hostage. Pennington surrendered to the police and was convicted to life in prison.
- Barry Loukaitis (14) was physically and verbally bullied at school, including an incident where one student held him down while another student urinated on him. After his family moved to a new community, Loukaitis became increasingly withdrawn and exhibited symptoms of psychiatric illness, taking several showers a day (Verlinden, Hersen, & Thomas, 2000). Loukaitis fantasized about a classroom attack after watching a movie about a teenager who held his algebra

class hostage. Loukaitis had easy access to guns. His parents kept firearms in the house. His family life was unstable. His parents were divorcing. Loukaitis not only witnessed his parents fighting, but also provided emotional support to his mother as she struggled with depression. On February 2, 1996, Loukaitis took a revolver, pistol, and handgun to Frontier Middle School in Moses Lake, Washington, where he held his algebra class hostage for 10 minutes before a gym coach intervened. Barry was sentenced to two life terms plus an additional 205 years in prison.

- Evan Ramsey (16) grew up in a series of foster homes, where he was physically and sexually abused. At Bethel Regional High School in Alaska, he suffered verbal bullying, including being called names, such as "retarded" and "spaz" (Verlinden, Hersen, & Thomas, 2000). Ramsey had access to an unlocked gun at home. He enjoyed playing violent video games and fantasized about killing certain people. On February 19, 1997, Ramsey attacked classmates in the commons area of his school. Other students knew of the plan and encouraged it, but never told any adult. After threatening suicide, Ramsey surrendered. He was sentenced to two terms of 99 years in prison.
- Luke Woodham (16) suffered name-calling and physical bullying at school. Psychiatrists described him as narcissistic and overly sensitive to insults (Verlinden, Hersen, & Thomas, 2000). His parents were divorced. His father was absent from his life and his mother vacillated between demanding and neglectful. A break-up with his girlfriend was the tipping point. Woodham became involved with a group of peers who played violent video games. The friends encouraged Woodham to seek revenge on his mother and girlfriend. On October 1, 1997, Woodham fatally stabbed his mother. He planned to take her gun, attack Pearl High School in Mississippi and to drive to Mexico. Woodham drove to Pearl High School where he fatally shot two people and injured seven. Woodham is serving three life terms plus an additional 140 years in prison.
- Michael Carneal (14) attended Heath High School in West Peducah, Kentucky, where he lived in the shadow of his sister, the class valedictorian and a popular student. Carneal was small for his age. His classmates found him rude and obnoxious and called him names, such as "nerd," "crack baby," and "freak" (Verlinden, Hersen, & Thomas, 2000). Carneal did outrageous things, such as selling parsley to classmates, claiming it was marijuana, and distributing pornography throughout the school. After the school newspaper printed a rumor that Carneal and another male student had feelings for each other, Carneal gathered a cache of weapons and ammunition. On December 1, 1997, Michael carried a gun to school and opened

fire on the school prayer group, killing three students and wounding three more. Carneal pleaded guilty and received a life term (25 years) in prison.

Historically, criminal penalties for school attackers have been very severe. Nicholas Elliott was sentenced to 114 years in jail, Barry Loutkaitis was sentenced to 205 years in jail, and Luke Woodham was sentenced to 140 years in jail. Most school attackers are tried as adults, which means they received harsher penalties than if they were tried as juveniles. No matter how much the school attacker was bullied or tormented, most attackers were not able to plea insanity because the prosecutors claimed that taking a weapon to school inferred premeditation, and premeditation contradicts a plea of insanity. Additionally, people like to think in very simple, dichotomous terms. Quick and easy assumptions are made that good people perform good actions and evil people perform evil actions. It is harder to comprehend ambiguity, where good people perform horrific actions. A deeper understanding of relationships, emotions, and situations that occur in life requires time, effort, and energy. Most people are unwilling to devote this type of energy and merely draw the conclusion that an evil act = an evil person. School attackers are quickly classified as evil and evidence that refutes this conclusion is discarded as irrelevant. Experiences, such as bullying victimization, are overlooked because they run contrary to the desired stereotype. Once the general public has drawn conclusions regarding a school attacker, reporters and investigators, prosecutors, and judges are susceptible to acting in ways that support public opinion. If public opinion demands a harsh penalty, judges are likely to mete out a harsh penalty. The lack of consistent victim responses to bullying also makes it difficult for people to fully understand the problem. Some children are resilient to bullying, others are not. It is difficult to explain why one victim picks up a gun and heads to school while another victim seems to shrug it off. Only those who are closest to the situation are able to see the school attacker as a complex individual who is both victim and offender.

One community which was able to see past demonizing an attacker was the Amish community of Pennsylvania. In 2006, Charles Carl Roberts IV, a 32-year-old milkman, attacked the West Nickel Mines Schoolhouse in Lancaster County. Roberts was home-schooled, so there was no history of bullying at school. Roberts was married with three children at the time of the attack. His attack was carefully planned. He targeted young girls, dismissing male students and adults before killing five girls and injuring five others. The motives for the killings remain unclear. Roberts, himself, reported that he was angry and frustrated over the death of his daughter. While barricaded in the schoolhouse, Roberts reported that he had molested two girls when he was pre-teen and was experiencing a drive to molest again. The confession could not be corroborated by his purported victims. As police stormed the building, Roberts committed suicide. After the shooting, the Amish community actively supported the families of the victims as well as Roberts's family. The community comforted Roberts's widow and parents immediately after the shooting and set up a memorial for families of the victims and the perpetrator. Together, the community grieved for the unnecessary loss of six lives. Outsiders were surprised by what seemed like an unusual response. Part of the reason why the Amish were able to forgive is because a core value of their faith is forgiveness. The Amish believe that a person cannot enter the Kingdom of Heaven unless the person has forgiven those who have caused hurt or affront. The other reason is that the Amish community is a very small and tight-knit community. Although Roberts and his family were not Amish, they were still considered neighbors and friends. The Amish were able to see beyond the evil nature of Roberts's final actions and consider the whole persona, a man suffering from post-traumatic stress disorder and delusional thinking. The Amish community provided a model for healing and recovery after the sudden and traumatic violence of school attack.

The 1999 attack on Columbine High School in Colorado shook the American public. Parents and educators could no longer believe that school attacks only happened in *those types of schools*. Columbine was an idyllic upper middle class community, far removed from the violence and venom of urban America. As three-time state football champions, athletes ruled the school. Teachers reportedly gave athletes preferential treatment, including allowing them to bully. On April 20, Eric Harris (18) and Dylan Klebold (17) attacked Columbine High School, killing 13 people and injuring 21 others, before turning the guns on themselves in a double suicide. Three students were injured attempting to escape. Multiple reasons have been given for the attack, including retaliation for bullying, excessive doses of violent video gaming and music lyrics, antisocial personalities, gothic-like culture, and narcissism. Possible causes of the Columbine tragedy have been argued and speculated about over and over again. Politicians and speakers have used Columbine as an example to emphasize various issues, including advocating for stricter gun laws, control of video game violence, banning certain types of music, and greater police presence in schools. The only real conclusions drawn from Columbine were that, if a school shooting could happen at a place like Columbine, school shootings could happen anywhere. This motivated the American public to ask serious questions about school shootings.

Because so many children are bullied while at school, it was initially difficult to distinguish bullying as a causal factor. Bullying victimization appeared to be a common trait experienced by most schoolchildren, attackers and nonattackers. The first insight into bullying as a causal factor came when the U.S. Secret Service investigated 37 school attacks (Vossekuil, Fein, Reddy, Borum, & Modzeleski, 2002). The key findings of the investigation were:

1) There is no typical profile of a school attacker.
2) Many attackers had access to a weapon prior to the attack.
3) Many attackers were victims of severe bullying prior to the attack. If the same bullying had occurred in the workplace, it would have met the legal definition of harassment or assault.
4) Many attackers were dealing with personal losses and contemplated suicide prior to the attack.
5) The attacks were not impulsive or sudden. Most attackers planned the incident.
6) Many attackers did not communicate a threat prior to the attack.
7) In cases where a threat was made, friends, family members, and classmates either did not take the threat seriously or encouraged the attack.
8) Those who knew about the plans did not communicate concerns to authorities because they did not trust authority figures to handle the matter appropriately.
9) Many attackers performed mild attention-seeking behaviors immediately prior to the attack and the presence of a caring adult in the attacker's life, someone that they could turn to for help, could have prevented many of the attacks.
10) The majority of the attacks ended within seconds, before law enforcement could get to the scene.

While one of the original objectives of the investigation was to profile school attackers, the investigators struggled to develop such a profile. There were few consistent patterns. There were no consistencies in family background. Some assailants lived with two parents, some lived with one parent, and some lived in foster homes. Academic success or failure was not a good indicator. Grades varied from good to struggling. A few attackers improved academic performance immediately prior to the attack. The attackers did not exhibit regular disciplinary problems. Two-thirds of the attackers had never been, or had rarely been, in trouble. One indicator was poor emotional health. Many assailants suffered from suicidal thoughts (78%) (Vossekuil, Fein, Reddy, Borum, & Modzeleski, 2002). This indicator was rarely identified by others. Only a few attackers had ever had a mental health evaluation (34%). Only 25 percent had a history of substance abuse. The main indicators that the investigators could come up with were a fascination with violence (59%), recent personal loss (98%), or victim of severe bullying (71%). The Secret Service report was instrumental in drawing the connection between a history of bullying victimization and school attacks.

Until Seung-Hui Cho's attack on Virginia Tech on April 16, 2007, college campuses seemed immune from school attacks. In 2007, Cho, a senior at Virginia Polytechnic Institute and State University in Blacksburg, Virginia, was nearing graduation and experiencing the stresses of a major life transition. Cho's troubles were complicated by his severe social anxiety and a history of clinical depression. As a child, Cho was very shy. He suffered selective mutism, a disorder where the affected person only speaks in particular situations and with select people. It is believed that Cho was bullied in middle school about his speech impediments. Cho's parents were open and progressive in seeking help for Cho. His parents helped him obtain psychiatric treatment, which continued throughout middle and high school. On graduation from high school, Cho attended Virginia Tech, where he majored in English. He was able to express his ideas in writing. During his junior year, his professors grew increasingly concerned about the topics of his essays. Neither Cho's parents nor professional counselors were contacted for assistance. On the day of the attack, Cho entered a dormitory at 7:15 A.M., where he shot a freshman female and the resident assistant who came to her aid. Some of the police force and security personnel who responded to the scene assumed that the shooting was an isolated incident, possibly the result of dating violence. This misconception gave Cho time for his next steps. Cho returned to his dormitory, changed his clothes, erased e-mail evidence, and removed his hard drive. At 9:00 A.M., Cho went to the post office, where he mailed a package to NBC News. The package contained personal essays revealing Cho's distorted mind and videos of Cho posturing with guns. Leaving the post office, Cho proceeded to a building with classrooms for science and engineering students. He locked the outside doors with chains and attached a note claiming that the chains were linked to a bomb that would detonate if the chains were tampered with. Cho then commenced his second attack, moving from classroom to classroom, shooting faculty members and students. As people in the building realized what was happening, several professors and students barricaded classroom doors or moved to offices for safety. Cho continued to attack, shooting through some of the barricades and returning to a couple of the classrooms for further devastation. After killing 32 people and injuring 17, Cho committed suicide. Six additional people were injured while attempting to escape. Cho's suicide note and documents sent to NBC News suggested that Cho felt rejected and persecuted by students with wealth. He saw himself as a savior of the oppressed and seemed to believe that his actions would make him a hero among others who were oppressed.

The Virginia Tech massacre exposed the vulnerabilities of college campuses to attack. A follow-up investigation identified ways to improve safety on college campuses and to provide a more comprehensive and coordinated response to attacks on campuses. The investigation criticized Virginia Tech security and administration for their failure to respond to faculty concerns regarding Cho's deteriorating mental health, failure to notify Cho's parents about changes in his mental health, failure to provide adequate counseling services, and delays in notifying students after the dormitory attack (Virginia Tech Review Panel, 2007). The State of Virginia was criticized for a lack of mental health resources and lax gun laws. The Virginia Tech Police Department was criticized for assuming that the first shooting was a case of intimate partner violence. Multiple recommendations developed from the incident, including procedures outlining a rapid response to campus emergencies and better communication with students, faculty, and staff at the start of campus emergencies.

Suicides and Bullying

Whereas homicide is aggression toward others, suicide is auto-aggression. Suicide seems contrary to the innate nature of any species. Throughout life, animals and humans struggle to stay alive. Intentionally ending one's life is the ultimate contradiction to the survival of the species. In attempting to identify why people contemplate or commit suicide, Durkheim (1897) identified four categories of suicides: egoistic, altruistic, anomic, and fatalistic. The types of suicide are differentiated by the suicide actor's self-image and degree of connection to society. In egoistic suicides, the actors are detached from society and have a limited ability to see or understand the views of others. People considering egoistic suicide carefully consider their own lives and circumstances and are upset if life seems to have no purpose or they seem to have no place in society. Durkheim observed higher rates of egoistic suicides among unmarried males and initially believed that egoistic suicides were a result of deterioration of family bonds. In altruistic suicides, individuals are too highly connected to their social group and unable to differentiate between personal needs for safety and security from the group's overall needs. Altruistic suicide actors do not value their life and are willing to die for the group's cause. Those who perpetrate suicide bombings engage in altruistic suicides. Anomic suicides are suicides that result from a disconnection with basic cultural values or norms. The high suicide rate among Native Americans is a good example of anomic suicide. As language, culture, and values are lost, individuals feel disconnected from their roots. Spiritual health is unstable. Life seems meaningless and with the loss of culture comes a loss of self-esteem. Fatalistic suicides are those where social standards and values are so strong that they oppress the individual's need for free self-expression. In fatalistic suicides, suicide actors see no hope for change. Examples of fatalistic suicides are the high rate of suicide by gay, lesbian, bisexual, and transgendered individuals. Various factors can increase the risk of suicide. Some of the main risk factors are low self-esteem, a history of self-harming behavior, mental illness, substance abuse, and easy access to guns. More recently, bullying has surfaced as a cause of youth suicide. Bullying can produce any of the various types of suicide, namely, egoistic, altruistic, anomic or fatalistic suicides.

Carl Joseph Walker Hoover transferred to the New Leadership Charter School in Springfield, Massachusetts, in sixth grade. He did not seem to fit in at his former elementary school and New Leadership promised a new start. His time at the new school was torturous. He did not seem to fit in at New Leadership, either. For over six months, Hoover was subjected to names and taunts. He reported the abuse to his mother, who met with school administrators many times, asking for help. The administrators were unresponsive and treated the abuse as an interpersonal dispute. They forced Hoover to eat lunch with his abuser for one week. The bullying continued. On April 6, 2009, just as his mother was getting ready to meet with school administrators once again, Hoover hung himself. His mother, a breast cancer survivor, described her son's emotional torment as worse than her battle with cancer.

Jaheem Herrera was a new student in the fifth grade at Dunaire Elementary School in Georgia. His family had recently emigrated from the Virgin Islands and Herrera was eager to make new friends. The children at Dunaire were not welcoming. They called him names, such as gay, ugly, and "the virgin." Herrera told his mother, who reported the bullying to school officials, an estimated seven or eight times. School officials were unresponsive and the bullying continued. Herrera concentrated on his schoolwork, earning decent grades. He did not do as well emotionally. He disengaged from the children at school. He was sad because he did not have any friends. On April 16, 2009, Herrera walked home from school, gave his mother his report card, went upstairs, and hung himself. Herrera needed a connection to supportive peers and Dunaire did not provide him with that connection.

Megan Meier was 13 years old when she took her life. Meier struggled with peer relationships from a young age. Friends seemed to come and go throughout her early childhood. While this was not unusual, Meier suffered from depression and attention deficit disorder, which made sustaining relationships a little more challenging for her. People with depression are not fun to be around and people suffering from attention deficit can be flighty and unfocused. It was difficult for Meier to develop and sustain peer relationships. As Meier reached adolescence, she wanted to connect with other teens, particularly seeking a potential partner or a date. Her past experiences and preexisting conditions made her vulnerable to superficial, insincere relationships. A former friend, the friend's 49-year-old mother, and the mother's 18-year-old employee saw Meier's desire to develop new friendships as an opportunity to embarrass Meier. The friend's mother was upset with how Meier and her daughter had broken off their relationship. There was nasty namecalling back and forth. The three decided to get back at Meier by developing an online relationship through a social networking site. The three used the pseudonym of Josh Evans and used a picture of a handsome young man. They wanted to lead Megan on, let her think that Josh was interested in her, and set up a meeting where the three would jump out, laugh, and humiliate Megan. They took turns posing as Josh Evans, exchanging messages with Megan and letting her think that Josh liked her. On October 16, 2006, the messages grew increasingly nasty. Josh told Meier that everyone in town hated her and that the world would be a better place without her. Meier responded by going to her room and hanging herself. Meier's parents did not know of the set-up until six weeks after Meier's suicide. Meier's mother now works with schools and business organizations to protect children on the Internet.

In 1998, students at McLoughlin Middle School in the state of Washington were being terrorized by a bully. The bully was so bold that he even attacked a child in front of the child's mother. The attack was so severe that the mother notified the police. The bully told police that the other child had thrown the first punch and the police did not pursue the incident any further. The mother believed that the police dismissed her complaint because her son's skin color was darker than the offender's skin color. On May 6, 1998, Jared High had the poor fortune to get trapped alone with the bully in the McLoughlin School gym. High had just called his brother to pick him up when he saw the bully. He braced himself, knowing that an attack was predictable and imminent. High was small. He knew that he could not win in a physical altercation with the larger child. He tried to stare the bully down but his tactic did not work. High tried calling for help but no one answered. The bully picked High up and threw him against the wall and floor, stomped on his shoulder, and punched him in the stomach. The assault continued for almost 10 minutes, with the bully taking breaks for a drink of water or to rummage through High's backpack. High managed to escape to the outside of the building. The bully followed, throwing High up against the brick wall, as henchmen cheered on the assault. The bystanders joined in the attack, calling High a wimp. When High's older brother arrived, he saw his brother's injuries and attacked the bully. The Vice Principal was called to investigate the bully's assault. The administrator questioned Jared with the bully present, a technique which can cause more harm to the victim. Administration blamed Jared for the assault. As a result of the assault, High experienced injuries to his stomach, back, shoulders, hips, and head. After the assault, he suffered from insomnia, nausea, loss of appetite, diarrhea, problems with the neck and spine, and noises in his head. Vomiting, loss of appetite, changes in sleep patterns, and mental changes are symptoms of concussion, a brain injury. Because Jared did not seek medical care immediately after the attack, administrators claimed that the injuries were unrelated to the attack. In addition to his physical injuries, High also complained of depression, a symptom of post-traumatic stress disorder. High's social and emotional state deteriorated until September 29, 1998, when he committed suicide. In order to prevent other suicides due to bullying, Jared's mother cofounded Bully Police USA, a watchdog organization that advocates for laws against bullying. The Bully Police website provides information on state laws and grades each state on 12 prevention criteria (bullypolice.org http://www.bullypolice.org/).

Jessica Logan thought that she had found her lifelong partner with whom she could share passion, intimacy, and commitment. While she was on spring break, she shared a nude photo of herself with her boyfriend, Ryan Salyers. When the couple broke up, Salyers forwarded the picture to four friends. The pictures were shared with other students at Sycamore High School. Logan was humiliated. She went to the school guidance counselor, who reported the incident to the school resource officer. The resource officer told the involved students to delete the pictures from their phones. Instead of deleting the pictures, the youth forwarded the pictures to other students. The photo was sent to hundreds of people, including students from three neighboring schools. Logan quickly became the target of vicious names and physical attacks, where students threw things at her during school. Logan went back to the school resource officer, reporting the escalation of incidents. He said that there was nothing that he could do. School gradually became unbearable. Logan was too embarrassed to share her mistake with her mother. She started skipping school to avoid the verbal abuse. The first indication Logan's mother had that something was wrong was when a truancy letter arrived from the school district. Logan told her mother what had happened. To ensure that Jessica attended school, her mother took her car away, and drove her to school. Logan's mom also offered to contact the offenders' parents. Logan declined the offer. She only had a few more weeks until graduation. Jessica seemed to be doing better. She had started sharing her experiences with others, warning teens not to share personal pictures. Logan talked with a local reporter in order to help other girls. Despite open and vicious harassment at graduation, Logan seemed to be improving. In July, a friend of

Logan committed suicide. After attending the funeral, Logan went home and hung herself. Since her daughter's suicide, Logan's mother has continued her daughter's advocacy, teaching teenagers about the potential consequences of sharing personal pictures.

Montana Lance was only nine-years-old when he hung himself inside the nurses' bathroom at Stewart Creek Elementary School in Texas. Lance had a learning disability and speech impediment. For two years, his classmates teased him about his disabilities and called him gay. When he reported the bullying to adults at Stewart Creek, his complaints were dismissed. He was told to stop being a tattle tale. When the bullying became too much for him to tolerate, he lashed out against the bullies. Getting sent to the school office became a regular occurrence. Lance's mother tried working with school staff to alleviate the problems. She reported the bullying to school staff. Her last complaint was made a week before Lance's death. On January 21, 2010, Montana Lance fought back against the bullying one final time. He was sent to the school office. As he had done in the past, Montana asked to use the nurses' bathroom and locked the door behind him. After about ten minutes, the nurse tried to open the door. Finding the door locked, she retrieved a key and found Lance unresponsive, without respirations or a pulse. The nurse attempted cardiopulmonary resuscitation. Lance's parents believe that he was too young to understand the irreversible nature of suicide. He may have been attempting to call attention to the problem, hoping a suicide attempt would be a wakeup call to adults. Lance's parents work now to prevent other youth suicides. They raise awareness through an annual event known as pink shirt day and an informative website with regular updates on bullying-related news events (http://www.pinkshirtday.ca/).

The Prince family emigrated from Ireland to South Hadley, Massachusetts, in search of a better life. South Hadley High School served a predominantly white, middle class population and was well known for their star football, lacrosse, and ice hockey teams. When Phoebe Prince (15) entered high school, she already had a history of bullying perpetration and self-harm behaviors from her previous school. Prince was one of several girls who had bullied a classmate in Ireland. The group used social networking sites to harass their victim with mean name-calling and nasty rumors. The underlying cause of the incident seemed to be jealousy. The target of Prince's bullying liked the same guy as Prince and her friends. In addition to the verbal abuse, Prince had a history of cutting herself, a self-harming behavior. On arriving at South Hadley, Prince briefly dated a star football player. After breaking up, Prince became the target for verbal abuse by the football player and a group of followers. At least five teens harassed Prince, calling her nasty names, scratching her pictures out of photos on the wall, and pushing her books out of her hands. Teachers knew of the abuse and did little, or nothing, to intervene. Prince tried to avoid school. On January 14, 2010, after a particularly hard day of being tormented, Phoebe went home and hung herself. The main ringleaders, nine students, faced varying charges of statutory rape, civil rights violations, disturbance of school assembly, criminal harassment, stalking, delinquency, and assault. The case became highly controversial in that it raised concerns about the role of overly aggressive prosecutors or district attorneys using bullying incidents to gain votes for political offices. Charges were brought against the youth, but not against the adults. Despite public demand, none of the school officials were charged with child maltreatment or neglect. In the end, five students were each sentenced to probation and approximately 100 hours of community service. Phoebe's death increased public awareness of the lack of bullying interventions in school and pressed Massachusetts legislators to develop antibullying laws.

Tyler Clementi (18) was a freshman at Rutgers University in Piscatawny, New Jersey. Like most college freshmen, Clementi was exploring his newly found freedom. Clementi was shy. It took a lot of courage for him to tell others that he was gay. Before starting university, Tyler told his roommate that he was gay. To avoid potentially embarrassing situations, Clementi told his roommate if he was going to bring a date back to the dorm. His roommate thought it would be funny to live stream a sexual encounter between Clementi and his date on the Internet. He invited others to watch. When Clementi learned of the violation, he contacted the Residence Assistant (RA) and two university officials. Tyler asked if he could move out. According to an Internet post, Clementi believed that the RA took his complaint seriously and intended to support his request. The assurances were not enough because, 15 hours later, on September 22, 2010, Tyler Clementi carefully placed his wallet on the side of the George Washington Bridge and plunged to his death. As a result of Clementi's death, New Jersey legislators passed the Anti-Bullying Bill of Rights Act, one of the toughest laws against bullying in the United States. The law requires school staff to undergo bullying prevention training and to investigate all reports of bullying.

No person deserves to feel degraded, humiliated, or hurt to the point where death is considered an appropriate solution. No person should be driven to the point where he or she can no longer think rationally. Suicide is not a solution, it is a problem. Suicide causes enormous pain for those who are left behind. Suicide robs friends, sisters, brothers, and parents of a loved one. The suicide of a son, daughter, girlfriend, boyfriend, niece, nephew, friend or classmate changes people for the rest of their lives. While some good may have come out of the premature and unnecessary deaths of Carl Joseph Walker Hoover, Jaheem Herrera, Megan Meier, Jared High, Jessica Logan, Montana Lance, Phoebe Prince, and Tyler

Clementi in that their deaths raised awareness of bullying as an issue and caused at least temporary changes in their schools, society will never know how much greater good could have occurred if these and other victims of bullycide had not succumbed to the petty and irresponsible behavior of others and decided to hold their heads high and continue to live a life of dignity and joy.

CHAPTER 2

The Definition of Bullying

Clear and consistent definitions of violence are important in medicine because they allow scientists to study and track health issues. If definitions of bullying varied, scientists would not be able to compare bullying in different periods of time, different populations, or different places. Having a standard definition that everyone agrees on allows comparisons that will help program developers to plan and evaluate programs. Bullying is defined as "when one or more persons with power repeatedly abuse a person with lesser power for the purpose of causing harm, distress, or fear." Bullying can occur directly, where the bully attacks the victim, or indirectly, where the bully instructs someone else, such as a henchman, to attack the victim. In order for an act to be considered bullying, the action must contain all components of bullying. The act must have (1) been done on purpose; (2) a malicious intent; (3) been performed repeatedly over time; and (4) involved an imbalance of power between the victim and the bully, where the bully has greater power. Malicious intent is defined according to the judgment of a reasonable person. If a reasonable person feels that the act could result in hurt, embarrassment, humiliation, or intimidation, the act meets the criteria of being malicious. The concept of repetition over time means that the bully attacks the victim over days, months, or years. The bully does not always perform the same action. Different forms of attacks may be used. The bully may start with subtle attacks, such as rolling eyes in disgust, and escalate to more obvious insults, such as hitting or verbal abuse. The important point is that the victim is targeted consistently over time. The attack is not a one-time event. The power imbalance is an important aspect of the definition because the power imbalance is what distinguishes bullying from other similar, childhood behaviors, such as immature social skills or rough play. The power imbalance tricks the bully into believing that it is alright to hurt the other person. The bully sees the victim as less than him or herself, not worthy of respect, and feels entitled to hurt the victim. The power imbalance is also what prevents bystanders from protecting the victim. Some onlookers are reluctant, or afraid, to stand up to someone with power.

An Imbalance of Power

Power is the degree of control that a person has over his or her social or physical environment. Power provides freedom. People with power have the freedom to decide where they want to live, work, and play, whom they want to associate with, and how they want to act. People can achieve power from many different sources. French and Raven (1959) identified the five main sources of power as: coercive power, legitimate power, reward power, expert power, and referent power. Power can be beneficial when it is used to help others or power can be detrimental as when it is used to hurt others. Positive examples of the use of power are the civil rights movements, when women, minorities, and people with disabilities achieved the same rights as others in society. Although a core value of American society is that all men are created equal, the United States still struggles to make equality a reality. At this time, homosexuals, new immigrants, and people who are poor still struggle with basic rights. Power is very deceiving. Those with power must know how to use it for good. When people with power use their power to hurt or humiliate others, it is often out of ignorance. The person who abuses power believes that power is constant. Power is not constant but is fluid and can move from person to person. As the civil rights movements demonstrated, a group of people may be belittled and put down at one time and can, later, rise up to take control. People with power are advised to use their power wisely, to benefit all, not just themselves. Bullies use their power to hurt the victim and to influence onlookers' reactions. If there is no power differential, the act is not bullying.

Coercive power is when someone forces another person to do something against his or her will. The stereotypical image of a large bully standing over a smaller child demanding lunch money is an example of someone abusing coercive power. In this case, the bully uses physical strength to make a provisional threat. Either the child gives the bully lunch money or the child is beaten up. Coercive bullies can threaten physical harm, injury with a knife or gun, violence against personal property, pets, or a loved one or they may use emotional threats, such as blackmail, or the threat of disapproval by the peer group. In order for coercion to be effective, the threat has to be credible. For example, if the smaller, weaker child threatens to beat up a larger child, the threat is not credible, and the coercion would be ineffective. In some cases, coercive bullies will demonstrate their force by hurting someone else in front of others. This public show of strength minimizes resistance by future victims and bystanders. Coercion is usually predatory, where the perpetrator is only acting for his or her own benefit. Coercive power has limitations because there is the possibility of being overpowered by a bully who is bigger or stronger.

Legitimate power is power given to people because of the position that they hold in society. People with legitimate power have the authority to establish rules and regulations and to determine who gets resources. Examples of people with legitimate power are teachers, school administrators, police officers, judges, and politicians. Some people, such as school disciplinarians, have a lot of power. They can control investigations, material that is produced as evidence against the accused students, and material that is overlooked. Just like corrupt police officers, school disciplinarians can frame an innocent student for an offense or let a guilty student off. The corruption of legitimate power begins when the person in a position of legitimate power does not understand the true nature of where the power originates. Legitimate power is deceptive. As a way to gain favor with the person in authority, people surrounding the authority figure will show feigned admiration. This respect can go to the head of people who are not smart enough to realize that their power comes from the position, and not from them, personally. People who are not wise enough to discern between true respect and feigned respect may start to abuse their power. In schools, the people with legitimate power are the school board members, superintendants, principals, assistant principles, disciplinarians, tenured teachers, police officers, and friends and family members closely associated with the aforementioned groups. Training programs for leaders may reduce or prevent some abuse of legitimate power. Anonymous and effective systems for reporting corruption can also reduce some abuse of legitimate power.

Reward power is the ability to control other people's actions through incentives or external motivators. Teachers, parents, and other childcare providers often use rewards to promote desired behaviors among children. When a teacher gives extra time at recess following good classroom behavior, the teacher is reinforcing desired classroom behaviors. Behavioral scientists have identified several ways that people use rewards, also called reinforcements. Positive reinforcement is the giving of a reward in order to increase the likelihood of a certain behavior. For a reward to be effective, the reward must be desirable to those who are receiving it. For example, rewarding children with extra homework is not likely to promote desirable behavior. Negative reinforcement is removing an undesirable experience. For example, if a child with asthma is having difficulty breathing, using an inhaler will alleviate the shortness of breath. The shortness of breath is the undesirable event and is removed through inhaler use. Many people confuse negative reinforcement with punishment. The difference between punishment and negative reinforcement is that negative reinforcement removes an undesirable stimulus whereas punishment adds an undesirable stimulus. The goal of negative reinforcement is to encourage a specific behavior. The goal of punishment is to stop a specific behavior or set of behaviors. In confusing negative reinforcement with punishment, adults may unintentionally model undesirable behaviors. For example, if a youth is using a cell phone in the hallway and the teacher takes the cell phone away from the student, the teacher is modeling an undesirable behavior—taking personal possessions without the owner's consent. Adults should be careful about what behaviors they wish to encourage among students, which behaviors they do not want, and model the behaviors that are desirable. Vicarious reinforcement is when people learn a behavior by watching another person successfully act out the behavior and receive an award for the behavior. The observers mimic the behavior that yielded the reward. Intermittent reinforcement is when the person earning the reward is reinforced sometimes and not at other times, with no particular pattern to the reinforcement. Intermittent reinforcement is believed to be the strongest type of reinforcement because it keeps the rewarded audience interested and engaged. They strive to enact the skill because they never know when they will receive the reward. Reward power can be abused when the person giving the rewards only gives rewards to friends, family members, or a select few members of the group. Taking away a reward once it is given is another way to abuse reward power. If rewards are unfairly meted out or taken away in a purposeful and intentional manner, the action may be synonymous with bullying. As with other forms of power, reward power has its limitations. The power of the reward is in the reward, not with the person providing the reward. If a second person comes along, offering a more valuable reward, the reward power is diminished. If the recipient becomes bored with the reward, the reward power loses potency. Rewards are useful for promoting positive behavior, when applied fairly and appropriately.

Expert power is the ability to control other people because of special knowledge, skills, or abilities. When people have a special knowledge of something, such as how the human body works, how to use or fix computers, or how to speak a second language, they can use this knowledge to help other people. Using knowledge to intentionally and repeatedly hurt another person is bullying. For example, the boss who withholds information about a project in order to interfere with an employee's performance is abusing expert power. Teachers who make students look stupid because they don't know an answer are abusing intellectual knowledge. A former friend who spreads nasty rumors abuses personal information. Any person who uses information to repeatedly belittle or humiliate another person is a bully. Intellectual bullying is difficult to identify because it is very easy to conceal. When questioned, abusers often attempt to cover up their behavior by claiming to have high standards. Claims are rarely questioned and the victims are viewed as being overly sensitive or complaining. There are ways to differentiate between high standards and intellectual abuse. If all students are held up to the same standards and treated with respect, the teacher is not a bully. If standards are variable and certain students are held up to higher standards than others and the higher standards could reasonably cause emotional distress to the targeted students, the actions may be labeled as bullying.

Persuasive language skills are a form of expert power. People who are skilled at verbal or written language have power, as conveyed in Edward Bulwer-Lytton's famous adage "the pen is mightier than the sword." Throughout history, language has proven to be more influential than any other power, including coercive or legitimate power. Linguistic power has been used to change people's perceptions, attitudes, and behaviors. Authors, poets, lawyers, and orators use words to stimulate changes. When Martin Luther King, Jr. stood on the steps of the Lincoln Memorial and addressed the audience with the words, "I have a dream that my four little children will one day live in a nation where they will not be judged by the color of their skin but by the content of their character," his words became pivotal to the civil rights movement. The words touched people in a way that coercion, laws, and political policies could not. The reason why words are more powerful is because words stimulate a desire for change that is motivated from within. Internal motivators are much stronger in achieving behavioral change than external motivators. People can use words for both good and bad reasons. On the negative side, words can be used to belittle, ridicule, humiliate, ruin reputations, and cause emotional pain. Yet, words only have power if the person receiving the words allows them to have power. Satire and trash talking are examples of the negative use of words where the receiver rarely allows the words to hurt or wound. In sports, trash talking is used to intimidate opponents and to throw players off their game. The reason why opponents may not become upset by the words is because the opponent understands that this is part of the game. There is a science to trash talking. The speaker must be able to time statements, improvise comments, and read the listener's body language, much like good comedians read an audience. Comedians know how to be quick witted and to hone in on minor characteristics. They also know when to back off when they have pushed the subject too far. Technology has changed linguistic power. Technology allows people who do not have strong language skills to take the time to develop and refine a message, giving the appearance that the person has better skills than they actually do. Technology limits the message sender's ability to read the listener and to know when the listener has been pushed too far. Technology allows the message sender to hide behind a screen of anonymity. Senders do not have to deal with immediate consequences of the message, which is to provoke upset or hurt the receiver. Modern technology provides expert power that can be, and is, easily abused.

Referent power is the ability to make others feel good about themselves. People are social beings and have an inherent need to feel desired, needed, and wanted as part of a social group. The need to belong is extremely apparent among youth who extend their social group in an attempt to identify an intimate partner. People who make others feel that they are special and belong to the group hold a lot of power. Referent power is particularly important in American adolescent society. Many people are filled with self doubt and feelings of inadequacy. The normal adolescent changes in body image cause a great degree of self doubt. Self-esteem is further assaulted by media images of flawless skin, the perfect body, or the ideal relationship. When reality does not match fantasy, some people become disillusioned. Some people have a natural skill for making others feel good. Coaches, mentors, teachers, friends who encourage and support have referent power. As with other sources of power, referent power may be used for good or for evil. The adults who bullied Megan Meier used their knowledge of young girls to lure Megan. The fictitious character "Josh" told Megan that she was beautiful. Megan was drawn into a relationship because she was struggling with her own issues of identity and friendships. What seemed to be a handsome young male was instead, a trap. Bullies use referent power. They lure naïve victims into a trap through compliments and, then, abuse the power when they have the victim in their grasp.

People obtain referent power from the social group. People with referent power tend to be popular and attractive. Popularity consists of two components: respect and likeability. Respect is admiration and tends to be mutual between the recipient of the respect and the person showing respect. An example of mutual respect is demonstrated when a famous actor or actress takes times to talk to fans, sign autographs, and makes each fan feel important. The actor or actress realizes that the fans provide power and there is a mutual respect between the artist and the fans. In some cases, respect is not mutual. The person receiving respect accepts, expects, or demands respect and gives none in return. The actor or actress may perceive fans as lesser beings, unworthy of attention or respect. This type of person tends to be egocentric, immature, and foolish because without the fan base, they would have no fame and respect. Bullies fit into the second category because the very act of bullying is a lack of respect. The bully fails to understand mutual respect. The second component of popularity—likeability—is based on physical attractiveness and personality. Researchers studying attractiveness have found that attractiveness varies by culture. In most cultures, faces and bodies that are symmetrical, balanced, and equal on both sides are perceived as more attractive. The desire for symmetry may have originated out of an aversion to disease. Some diseases, such as syphilis or traumatic brain injuries, can produce facial asymmetry. In American culture, faces that are either strongly masculine or strongly feminine are deemed more attractive. Males are considered more attractive if they have a wide jaw, large chin, wide mouth and nose width, narrow lip line, bushy eyebrows, and small eyes. Whereas females who have a small jaw, small chin, small mouth and nose width, full lips, thin eyebrows, and large eyes are considered more attractive. Because these gender differences are determined by the sex hormones—androgen (in males) and estrogen (in females)—adult facial structure is not reached until after puberty. This means that youth who progress through puberty significantly earlier than peers may have greater referent power in the school community. For example, the 15-year-old male who is still in seventh grade will have a great deal of influence over other males in his class. For those who do not have strongly masculine or strongly feminine facial structures, there is hope. Dating partners are selected on many factors that extend beyond attractiveness. Homogamy, how much the couple have the same features—hair color, facial structure, height, and intelligence—is more important to the success and stability of a relationship than physical attractiveness. Referent power, making others feel good about themselves, is a valuable trait. However, as with other forms of power, referent power can change over time and with circumstances.

Bullying is an imbalance of power and, in some cases, power imbalances are clear. The older, larger bully who takes lunch money from a younger child clearly has coercive power. The school disciplinarian who punishes a specific student more harshly than others is abusing legitimate power. The girlfriend who spreads nasty rumors is abusing expert power. Determining the degree of power that one has is like a complex mathematical equation and the comparisons become even more difficult when trying to figure out who holds the greater power in interpersonal interactions. Siblings are one example of how power differentials are not always clear. An older sibling may have greater physical strength. However, the younger sibling may have knowledge of the older sibling's vulnerabilities, such as a fear of spiders, concerns about a birthmark, or desire for a girlfriend or boyfriend. The younger child may use this expert power to attack the older one in ways that can cause profound hurt. Power has many components which can alter drastically under seemingly minor circumstances. Perceptions of power can be deceiving. A bully may believe he or she has greater power, only to find that the victim has a discrete power which is much greater than the bully's power. In some cases, giving up power can lead to more power because empowering others provides referent power.

Purposeful and Chronic

The second component of the definition of bullying is that the act is done to intentionally hurt the victim. If a person stretches his or her leg out and a passing person trips over the foot, the action may or may not be bullying, depending on whether the first person meant to inflict injury. While the act of sticking a leg out may have been intentional, inflicting hurt may not have been intended. In considering intent, it is important to consider the developmental age of the children involved. At recess, young children, of ages 5–7 years often play tag, a game of hitting and running. To this age group, hitting and running is play, not intended to hurt anyone. They lack the skills to play organized games, such as softball or basketball. Middle school youth also demonstrate a "hit and run" behavior when they are trying to get the attention of someone whom they are physically attracted to. They lack communication skills needed to converse and interact with potential dating partners. This lack of social skills can unintentionally cause hurt. The behaviors mimic bullying actions, but lack the malicious intent of true bullying.

The next component of the definition of bullying is that the malicious behavior is repeated over time. The bully may not perform the same behavior and may change behaviors. However, the actions are malicious and intended to cause harm to the victim. In some rare cases, one incident is still sufficient to categorize the behavior as bullying. The one-time incident concept was first recognized in workplace bullying, where the first act of bullying is so severe that the victim knows not to fight back. New employees are particularly vulnerable because when new employees first enter the workplace, they are still learning company values. If a bully attacks, the newcomer will often submit to the bullying. One reason for submission may be that co-workers are still learning the personality traits of the new employee and to complain about bullying the first week or two on the job may reflect poorly on the newcomer. A second reason is that the newcomer may believe that bullying is the organizational norm. In some companies, senior managers bully junior managers and junior managers bully frontline staff. The newcomer may believe that subjecting oneself to chronic abuse is the price of working for the organization. The newcomer also may not know the correct policy for reporting or may not trust human resources to act in ways that will protect new workers. The final reason for bullying only requiring one incident is that some people are quick learners. The workplace bully may be demonstrating his or her higher position in the organization. Respecting the hierarchy makes life easier for the victim. For the most part, bullying is repeated over time. In some special and severe cases, bullying may be a one-time incident.

Confusion with Other Harmful Behaviors

Not every incident of hitting, kicking, threatening, name-calling, or intimidating is bullying. Incidents of play-fighting, wrestling, verbal jousting, and mutual teasing are not bullying if both parties are willing participants and both parties have equal power (Olweus, 1993). Play-fighting, trash talking, and teasing are pseudo-bullying. They appear to be bullying but lack the intention to cause harm and an imbalance of power. Pseudo-bullying can quickly cross the line into true bullying if one party becomes angry or frustrated and suddenly desires to cause harm. Mock bullying, where two or more youth pretend to bully, is also not bullying. Mock bullying is rare but has been reported in schools where teachers provide rewards to bystanders for breaking up bullying incidents. In these cases, students will stage bullying incidents in order to attain rewards.

Interpersonal conflict where both parties have equal power is not bullying. Interpersonal conflicts occur between dating partners, married couples, friends, work colleagues, neighbors, and governments and are a normal part of life. When people disagree over an issue, it is usually an issue that they care greatly about. Issues that people don't care about do not arouse controversy. In this way, conflict is a good thing. Conflict means that people are engaged and interested in issues. Topics that cause controversy tend to be issues of personal opinion, that is, who is the best quarterback, which is the fastest racecar, the best college to attend, best restaurants, how to allocate teamwork fairly, or the value of someone's time. Issues that are factual, that is, which quarterback has the highest quarterback rating or which car has the fastest lap time on the Nürburing Nordschleife track, are less likely to cause controversy. The danger of confusing interpersonal conflict with bullying is that the solutions are very different. Interpersonal conflicts can be resolved peacefully through face-to-face negotiations, mediation, or litigation. The end result is some form of compromise by both parties. The compromise may require a third party to act as an arbitrator. With bullying, there should be no compromise. The victim should not have to accept any form of abuse. The victim should not have to negotiate for basic rights of safety. Additionally, because bullying involves an imbalance of power, bullies can easily persuade arbitrators to pressure victims into accepting the bullying. Differentiating between interpersonal conflicts and bullying is important to ensure that victims' rights are protected.

Harassment, assault, child maltreatment, and Intimate Partner Violence (IPV) are not bullying. Harassment, child maltreatment, and some forms of IPV are actions that cross legal and social boundaries, and are classified as criminal behavior. The legal definitions of criminally violent acts vary from state to state. Harassment is usually defined as offensive threats, ridicule, insults, comments, physical advances, gifts, letters, communication or attention that, according to the judgment of a reasonable person, is intended to cause fear, intimidation, oppression, or persecution. In workplace law, harassment is limited to offenses based on race, skin color, nationality, religious preference, gender, sexual orientation, disability, or retaliation for not accepting abusive behaviors. In order to count as harassment, the actions must be severe enough to cause a hostile or offensive workplace. Battery is a type of violence where force is used with the intention of hurting another person. Battery can be committed through direct contact, such as hitting or kicking a person, or indirectly, such as throwing a rock or pushing an object or person into someone else. Assault is attempted battery, where the perpetrator attempts to use force in order to hurt another person. Child maltreatment is the abuse or neglect of a child by a parent or caregiver. Caregivers are defined as coaches, teachers, clergy, or other adults in a custodial role of caring for someone under the age of 18 years. Child maltreatment may be physical, sexual, emotional abuse, or due to neglect. Depending on state laws, bullying can be a form of child maltreatment, if the bully is a legal adult and the victim is a minor, under the age of 18 years. IPV is physical, sexual, or psychological violence or the threat of violence by a current or former dating partner or spouse. The couple does not need to have had sexual relations in order for violence to be considered IPV. IPV can occur between heterosexual or same-sex partners, whether they have had sex or not. Depending on the type, severity, and frequency of violence, harassment, assault, IPV, and child maltreatment are punishable as misdemeanors or felonies.

It is important to differentiate bullying from other acts of violence because classifying acts of severe violence as bullying minimizes the significance of some violent acts. Assault is a criminal offense. Classifying an assault as bullying misdirects the public in how to best handle the offense as perpetrators are set free and do not experience any consequences for criminal actions. Likewise, classifying bullying as assault can initiate systems that are either ineffective for dealing with bullying or cause more problems. The American criminal justice system already has severe inequalities and injustices, where youth who are poor, have dark skin, or are uneducated are more likely to receive harsher penalties than people who are wealthy and educated. Approximately 50 percent of high school students report bullying another child. If every high school student who bullies another child is incarcerated, there would be a lot of children in jails and detention centers. On the other side of the argument, children have the right to feel safe at school. If bullying advances to such a degree where the child suffers physical or emotional harm, it is only appropriate for adults to follow laws regarding harassment or child maltreatment. This path should be combined with a strong warning. If adults in a community use the legal system to control even one bully, they must be prepared to use the legal system for all other bullies, including bullies with legitimate power, such as the school board president's son or daughter, the overly zealous school police officer, or the selectively and harshly punitive school disciplinarian.

Bystander Behavior

Bullies depend on bystanders to behave in certain, expected ways. If bystanders do not act in the ways that the bully expects, the bullying is thwarted and the bully might look silly or stupid. The Bullying Circle was developed by Dr. Olweus to describe the different roles that bystanders act out during bullying incidents (Olweus et al., 2007). The *bully* acts as the alpha leader, the person in charge of the group. Others in the group act as hunters, lookouts, or caretakers of the victim. *Follower henchmen* are the members of the group who ally with the bully. Follower henchmen actively and aggressively participate in the attack. They can either lead the attack or act under spoken or unspoken directions from the bully. Henchmen are rarely aggressive toward each other, which suggests that henchmen honor the social group. They differentiate between who is in and who is out of the group. Some experts believe that the follower henchmen receive some type of social benefit by aiding the bully. The henchmen may experience an upgraded status within the group as a result of helping the bully. *Supporter henchmen* cheer on the attack or congratulate the bully and/or henchmen after the attack. This conveyance of respect, whether real or feigned, boosts the bully's ego and fuels future attacks, providing positive reinforcement to the bullying behaviors. *Passive supporters* or *cosigners* indirectly encourage aggression by watching the bully and henchmen. The bully and henchmen misinterpret the passive supporters' interest as admiration. The attention feeds the bully's ego. Passive supporters rarely get into trouble for failing to act. They simply walk away, feigning ignorance. *Disengaged onlookers* watch with indifference. This group also does not get involved and bullies will assume that the failure to get involved means that the bullying is supported or warranted. Some teachers and adults will act as disengaged onlookers, particularly if the victim is a child whom they dislike or find irritating. *Possible defenders* are those bystanders who do not like the violence and want to help the victim, yet do not. Possible reasons for the lack of action, or helping the victim, may be a lack the knowledge of how to safely intervene, fear of provoking the bully and making the situation worse for the victim, or fear of becoming the bully's next target. Possible defenders experience cognitive dissonance, a feeling of emotional upset, because their actions are contrary to their core values. Cognitive dissonance impacts spiritual health, the feeling that values and actions are consistent or inconsistent. The *Defenders* group is altruistic. They help the victim by telling the bully to stop the bullying, reporting the bullying to an adult, helping the victim get away from the situation, or diverting the bullies' attention to something else. Defenders put their own needs for safety and social acceptance aside for the sake of the victim. Bullying can only occur when henchmen, supporters, and disengaged onlookers outnumber the possible and actual defenders. If the number of defenders is higher than the bully and henchmen, bullying incidents either will not occur or will end very quickly. The Bullying Circle is integral to bullying.

Forms of Attack

Injury can be inflicted directly, by the bully, or indirectly, by the bully telling the henchmen to hurt the victim. The four main modes of attack are *physical,* such as hitting, pushing, brushing up against, kicking, or taking personal items without permission; *verbal or nonverbal,* such as name-calling, cyber bullying, gestures, nasty looks, or insults; or *psychological,* such as putdowns, threats, exclusion from the social group, spreading rumors, or by manipulating authorities to punish the victim for a false or exaggerated offense. Bullies usually start with subtle or covert behaviors, such as invading personal space, asking an inappropriate question, rolling eyes, taking without permission, or ignoring. Crossing these small boundaries allows the bully to see how the victim and bystanders will react. If the victim or bystanders react strongly, criticizing the action, the bully may back down. The use of discrete boundary violations also produces uncertainty in the victim and observers. Adults or potential defenders will question whether the action was truly malicious or intentional. By using ambiguous actions, the bully can claim that the action was unintentional or that the victim is overly sensitive. If the victim ignores the attack or does not call the bully on the behavior, the bully interprets this as acceptance or passivity. Some bullies remain satisfied with discrete, annoying attacks, while other bullies will escalate to more overt, obvious behaviors, such as assault or manipulating authorities to punish the victim.

Bullying behaviors can be classified by the trajectory of the attacks over time (Broidy et al., 2003; Marsee & Frick, 2007). Covert attacks that increase over time are low and increasing. Covert attacks that decrease over time are low and decreasing. Covert attacks that are stable over time are low and stable. Overt attacks that increase over time are high and increasing. Overt attacks that decrease over time are high and decreasing. Overt attacks that are stable over time are high and stable. Classifying the levels and trajectories of attacks can help to determine current and predicted future severity.

Physical Bullying

Physical bullying is one of the more commonly recognized forms of bullying. Physical bullying includes pushing, hitting, slapping, kicking, nudging, spitting, tugging on hair, stepping on someone's toe, tripping, inappropriate touching, or throwing an object at the victim. Physical bullying also includes actions that deprive a person of their personal belongings, such as stealing, taking items without permission, failing to return an item, intentionally damaging an item, or coercing someone to give a gift. The consequences of physical bullying are physical and emotional injuries and financial loss. Behaviors are often based on the developmental age of the perpetrator. Hitting, pushing, or kicking tend to be more common in younger children. Children in kindergarten and first grade commonly engage in random, unorganized, active play. Bullies can use such activity to hide maliciousness. Physical bullying takes a lot of energy. It is difficult and exhausting for one bully to perpetrate a prolonged physical attack. Thus, bullies who use physical attacks may either need to recruit henchmen or will use short, limited-duration attacks.

Verbal and Nonverbal Bullying

Name-calling is the most common form of bullying. Children are humiliated with rude names or nasty comments about clothes, shoes, teeth, color or texture of skin, hair, make-up, cultural or ethnic background or sexual orientation. Messages can be transferred verbally or nonverbally through letters, notes, or electronic messages. In addition to the humiliation of direct verbalizations, victims may be the target of obscene gestures, nasty looks, rolling of the eyes, or other expressions of dislike or put-down. Often given a category by itself, cyber bullying is a technologically advanced form of verbal bullying. Cyber bullying includes e-mails, instant messages, text messages, and electronic postings that express hurtful messages. Tactics used by cyber bullies involve using vulgar and offensive language to hurt another person, posting cruel gossip or rumors, posting secret and embarrassing information about someone else, intentionally excluding someone from an electronic list, posing as someone else online in order to deceive, cyber stalking, or tricking someone into sharing personal information (Willard, 2009). Cyber bullying is often an extension of bullying that starts in the school or community. Cyber bullying enables a greater degree of hurt because the bully is shielded by perceptions of invisibility.

Bullies use a wide variety of ways to hurt their victims. Cyber bullying is especially harmful because the bullies do not see the victim's reaction and are unable to judge the degree of hurt done to the victim. (Yuri Arcurs/Shutterstock.com)

The electronic medium shields the perpetrator from face-to-face interaction with their victims. There is a lack of tangible feedback which would normally guide good decision-making (Willard, 2009). Bullies are unable to judge the victim's breaking point. It is easier to underestimate the emotional damage done to a victim. The bully can also hide behind a screen of anonymity, limiting retaliation by the victim. Thus, cyber bullying can be a very severe form of nonverbal bullying. Not all online aggression is bullying (Wolnack, Mitchell, & Finkelhor, 2007). When the bully and victim do not know each other and the balance of power is unknown, the action may be an interpersonal conflict caused by differences of opinion, and does not amount to bullying. As technology advances, other modes of bullying will continue to develop.

Psychological Bullying

Psychological bullying are actions that are intended to result in embarrassment, humiliation, indignity, grief, or emotional upset to the victim.

Common forms of psychological abuse involve excluding a person from the group, giving someone an ugly glare, spreading nasty rumors, depriving a person of needed resources so that the person has to ask or beg for assistance, getting someone into trouble by providing false information or exaggerating a minor offense, threatening to hurt someone, or forcing someone to do something against his or her free will. Spreading nasty and hurtful rumors fits within two categories. Rumor mongering is both verbal bullying and psychological bullying. Because of the emotional implications, spreading nasty rumors is traditionally considered emotional abuse. Psychological bullying is a subtle form of abuse and difficult to detect. Psychological abuse requires little physical energy and can continue aggressively for long periods of time, without respite for the victim. Adults and bystanders may unintentionally go along with the bullying if they believe that the rumors are true or that the victim deserves the bullying. Psychological abuse is easier to perpetrate if bystanders already hold stereotypes about the victim. For example, if a group of females reports a male provocative victim for fighting back when they called him names, the teacher or administrator who has stereotypes that girls are good and boys are bad may easily go along with punishing the male. Misperceptions regarding the relationship between the bully and the victim can also unknowingly support psychological abuse. If bystanders believe that the bully and victim are friends, they will assume that the rumors originating from the bully are true. If the bully is perceived as someone with personal insight into the victim's life, rumors are likely to continue to circulate. Bystanders are reluctant to get involved because they believe that the actions are simply an interpersonal dispute between two friends. What bystanders do not realize is that, by failing to get involved, they are playing into the bullying. They are acting as passive supporters.

Workplace bullying deserves special mention as a form of bullying because workplaces enable bullies to engage in specific types of bullying, typically emotional bullying. Schools are workplaces and some of the bullying behaviors seen in workplaces may be seen in schools too. Workplace bullying is usually very subtle and hard to detect because the bully does not want to risk disciplinary action or loss of income. Signs of an abusive workplace could be a biased interpretation of rules, unjustified criticism, or fault finding for minor mistakes. Bosses who bully use the organizational structure and policies to bully. They will apply policies more leniently to favored employees and more harshly to employees they dislike. They will draw middle level employees into the bullying as henchmen. Other signs of workplace bullying are giving unclear or contradictory work instructions, withholding information that is necessary for work completion, isolating the target from colleagues, and ridiculing the target's work in front of others. If noticed by upper management, the bullying behaviors may be misconstrued as poor leadership skills. It is possible to differentiate abusive behaviors from poor leadership. When someone in a position of power exaggerates mistakes, while purposefully ignoring or minimizing accomplishments of the victim, it amounts to bullying. The boss who knowingly gives credit for stellar work to a person who didn't perform the work is a bully. The ongoing emotional abuse of workplace bullying leads to feelings of frustration or outrage by the victim. Many victims disengage. They no longer care about productivity or success because they expect their success will be met with further punishment. Disengagement may be expressed as disinterest, poor performance, feigned illness, or in schools, as truancy.

The different forms of bullying—physical, verbal, and emotional—are not mutually exclusive. The various forms of bullying can be combined. For example, sending a nasty message about someone and then "accidently" forwarding it to the victim is both verbal and emotional abuse. Bullies seem to develop and refine an endless arsenal of ways to hurt victims. As one mechanism is shut down, other strategies for bullying emerge. This is why it is important to focus on all the interactions between the victim, bully, and bystanders, and not just on one specific action or set of actions.

CHAPTER 3

Prevalence

An estimated 1.6 million children in grades 6–10 are bullied each week in the United States (U.S. Department of Justice, 2001). It is difficult to comprehend a number this size or to understand the extent of the problem without knowing the total number of children in grades 6–10 in the United States at the time of this estimate. Prevalence is a statistic describing the number of people affected by a problem at a given point in time divided by the total number of people in the population at the same point in time. Prevalence rates provide a better understanding of the problem because they are standardized numbers where both the numerator and the denominator are known. Prevalence rates of bullying victimization and perpetration allow comparisons between places, genders, and time periods, which is much more useful than raw numbers.

In 1997–1998, the World Health Organization (2002) studied bullying among 13-year-olds to determine the prevalence of bullying in different countries. The study found that 35 percent or 35 out of 100 students in the United States reported involvement with bullying, sometimes or more often. Countries with the highest bullying rates were Austria (64/100), Germany (61/100), Denmark (59/100), Greenland (57/100), Lithuania (57/100), and Switzerland (53/100). The United States ranked 15th, below Israel with 36/100 students and above Finland with 33/100 students. The lowest rates of bullying were found in Sweden (12/100), England (14/100), Greece (19/100), Wales (20/100), and Northern Ireland (21/100). The WHO data are limited in that the surveys only measured youth involved in bullying. The researchers did not separate out which children were bullies and which children were victims. In a national study, Nansel et al. (2001) studied prevalence rates of bullies and victims to find that 13/100 of students were bullies, 11/100 were victims, and 6/100 were both bullies and victims, a group known as provocative victims.

It is important to use common definitions when comparing prevalence rates. Most researchers use a time frame of victimization (or perpetration) within the past couple of months. Longer timeframes, such as lifetime bullying rates, the number of youth bullied at some time in their entire lifetime, yield higher numbers (90–100/100). As researchers refine techniques and agree to standard definitions, estimates of prevalence rates become increasingly more accurate. Currently, approximately 50/100 students in the United States report bullying perpetration and 48/100 report victimization (Josefson Institute, 2010).

Differences by Age and Gender

Bullying victimization appears to decline from the third to the seventh grade. A study of more than 9,000 students found that 55/100 third graders, 46/100 fourth graders, 40/100 fifth graders, 34/100 sixth graders, and 29/100 seventh graders reported victimization (Tsafos, Black, & Washington, 2008). If the prevalence of victims decreases as youth age, experts predict that the prevalence of bullies should also decrease. This is, however, not the case. Bullying perpetration rates increase from 8/100 in third and fourth grades to 18/100 in seventh grade. Experts believe that victimization rates do not truly decrease with grade progression. It is more likely that the numbers reflect social values. By eighth grade, most youth do not want to be considered a victim because victims are perceived as weak, and are rejected by society. Youth prefer to view themselves as the stronger one, the bully. Thus, the changes in victimization and perpetration rates may reflect changes in social attitudes and perceptions. The types of bullying may change as well. Older youth may use more subtle, discrete forms of bullying. The prevalence of bullying probably remains the same throughout the grade levels.

There are gender differences in types of bullying but not as many as some people believe. The most common forms of victimization are name-calling (36%), physical bullying (18%), relational exclusion (15%), rumors (14%), nasty comments of a sexual nature (13%), nasty comments about race or ethnicity (10%), theft (5%), and nasty comments about religious affiliation (5%). Overall, females and males have similar rates of victimization; 48 percent of females and 53 percent of males report victimization. Males are more likely to experience name-calling (38%), physical bullying (23%), and social exclusion (17%), whereas females report higher rates of rumor mongering (15%) and sexual comments or gestures (15%). So, while society typically thinks of social exclusion as a female form of bullying, social exclusion is just as common among males and, in some communities, more common.

High-Risk Groups

Children who are new to a community, children with disabilities, children with learning disorders, children with mental health disorders, and youth who are lesbian, gay, bisexual, or transgendered (LGBT) report higher rates of victimization than other children. The inability to make and maintain friends is an underlying factor that places all of these youth at risk of victimization. Children without friends are three times more likely to be bullied by nasty rumors, two and a half times more likely to be excluded from a group, and twice as likely to experience physical bullying and name-calling (Black, Weinles, & Jackson, 2007). Children who are new to a community may have trouble breaking into already established social groups. The social groups are satisfied as they are and do not actively seek or welcome new members. To compound the problem, children from a different region or country may speak in a dialect or accent that is not familiar to classmates. Immigrants may practice different customs of behavior or bring an ethnic food to school for a snack. Different behaviors make a child stand out. If the school population is homogeneous and rigid, it is harder to accept those who are different. The child may be accepted, or rejected, depending on the openness of other

Approximately 10 percent of students are bullied at school. Youth who are new to a school, have unique traits, or who represent a minority group are at greatest risk of victimization. (Oliveromg/Shutterstock.com)

students and the teachers. Heterogeneous schools, with diverse populations, are easier to integrate into than schools with homogeneous, well-established populations. Newcomers are easy targets for bullies. Some bullies may use the need for socialization as a way to gain the victim's trust and set the victim up for bullying. By pretending to be a friend, the bully can learn personal secrets that could later be used as ammunition to hurt the victim. The feigned friendship also conceals the behaviors. The bully can claim that the behavior was a joke or just a way to initiate the victim into the social group. Children who are new to a community will require adult help to integrate into the community and supervision during integration to protect against unhealthy relationships with potential bullies.

Children with special needs are those with physical or mental health disorders that require medical intervention. Children with special needs are at higher risk of victimization due to a variety of factors, such as obvious physical and behavioral differences caused by the disease, time away from school, or pre-existing emotional stress due to chronic illness. A large scale study showed that children with special health needs were victims and perpetrators of bullying significantly more than children without special health needs (Van Cleave & Davis, 2006). Forty percent of children with special health needs reported victimization, in comparison to 32 percent of children who did not have special health needs. Thirty percent of the children with special health needs reported bullying others, in comparison to 21 percent of children without special health needs. Among children with special health needs, 15 percent reported provocative victimization in comparison to 9 percent of children without special health needs. Of children with special health needs, children with behavioral, emotional, or developmental problems reported the greatest rate of victimization, with 55 percent reporting victimization.

Obesity, cancer, speech and language impairments, visual problems, diabetes, attention deficit hyperactivity disorder (ADHD), psychiatric and nervous problems are just some of the disorders that increase risk of bullying victimization. The rate of bullying victimization is three times higher for children with cancer (Lahteenmaki, Huostila, Hinkka, & Salmi, 2002), three times higher for children with speech and language problems (Conti-Ramsden & Botting, 2004), nine times higher for children with psychiatric problems, and ten times higher for children with ADHD (Nordhagen, Nielson, Stigum, & Kohler, 2005). Males who are obese are 1.7 times more likely to be bullies and 1.5 times more likely to be victims. Females who are obese are 1.5 times more likely to be bullies (Griffiths, Wolke, Page & Horwood, 2006). Maintaining optimal physical and emotional health and having systems in place for children with special needs is important to reduce bullying in schools.

Youth who are lesbian, gay, or have gender ambiguity due to genetic or chromosomal aberrations are also at risk of victimization. Children as young as those in pre-school engage in play that is gender-specific, girls mimic female roles in society and boys mimic male roles. A child who does not fit gender expectations can make others feel uncomfortable. Approximately 2 percent of youth self-report as gay or lesbian, 7 percent as bisexual, and 4 percent as not sure of their sexual orientation. This means that homosexual and bisexual youth account for almost one out of ten youth. Youth who are lesbian, gay, bisexual, or transgendered (LGBT) face numerous social disadvantages. LGBT people live with expectations of abuse, knowing that negative stereotypes exist and, yet, never knowing when, how, or by whom prejudices will be expressed. Approximately 8 out of 10 LGBT youth report experiencing verbal harassment; 4 out of 10 report experiencing physical harassment, and 2 out of 10 report experiencing physical assault within the past year at school (Kosciw Greytak, Diaz, & Bartkiewicz, 2010). Six out of 10 LGBT youth do not feel safe at school (Kosciw Greytak Diaz & Bartkiewicz, 2010). LGBT youth are at much higher risk for school truancy, dropping out, and suicide. LGBT youth are more than two times as likely to attempt suicide as straight peers and, of those who do attempt suicide, twice as many wanted to die (Russell & Joyner, 2001). Social acceptance plays a major role in the suicidal ideation of LGBT youth. One study showed that LGB youth who are rejected by their family are eight times more likely to attempt suicide in comparison to LGB youth who are accepted by their family. Youth who question sexual orientation are more adversely affected by bullying than those who have come out. Family, community, and social supports, such as Parents, Families, and Friends of Lesbians and Gays (PFLAG), combined with positive depictions of LGBT youth in the media, can protect LGBT youth from bullying and, ultimately, suicide.

Many children experience social exclusion at school. It is important to note that having a different skin color, speaking with an accent, or sexual orientation does not justify the humiliation and pain of bullying victimization. The problem lies with the rigidity of the social group, not with the individual characteristics of the child. Because bullying is a social disorder, high-risk groups depend on the community's preferred character or personal traits. If people in a community define a behavior or trait as unacceptable, individuals with that trait are more easily bullied, ridiculed, or excluded because others in the community are reluctant to stand with them. It is important to remember that the same trait that is rejected or ridiculed in one society may be welcomed by another group. Throughout his life, civil rights activist Ed Roberts (1935–1995) demonstrated the idea that society defines what is normal and what is abnormal, what traits are welcomed and what traits are rejected. Ed Roberts was an active, healthy youth, playing baseball and hanging out with friends. At the age of 14, Roberts contracted polio, a viral disease that causes paralysis and, often, death. It was two years before Salk discovered the polio vaccine and Roberts almost died. Roberts spent 18 months in an iron lung, a huge, heavy chamber that forced his lungs to expand and contract. He was only able to survive outside of the iron lung for a few hours a day. His body withered. He lost weight, developed muscle contractures, and suffered from depression. His mother, Zona, encouraged Roberts to achieve all that he could. She made him continue his school studies by participating in classes via the telephone. As Roberts's health stabilized, his mother insisted that he attend school at least once a week. He could stay off the iron lung for a few hours at a time. But, his breathing was awkward and poorly controlled. It took all of the muscle strength that he could muster to gasp for breath. Roberts was horrified of what other students would think of him. They would stare at him. They would surely make fun of him. Roberts was at high risk of bullying. On arriving at school, Roberts realized that the other students were curious. They knew him as the voice at the end of the telephone line, the student who had attended classes from home. Now they had a face to connect with the voice. Roberts could either hide from his classmates or he could embrace the attention. Roberts decided to embrace the fame and became a celebrity in his school. Roberts's experiences in high school taught him strength, conviction, and dignity. On graduation, Roberts wanted to attend a four-year college. As an invalid, he should have been eligible for support by the California Department of Rehabilitation. On reviewing his case, the department concluded that it was unlikely that Roberts would ever work or become a productive member of society. It was decided that supporting his education would be a waste of resources. Roberts found sympathetic support from a counselor at his local community college and the local press. He attended and graduated from community college and later continued onto the University of California at Berkeley. He initially lived in the student health department because the dormitory floors could not support his iron lung. The news quickly spread that a quadriplegic was living and studying at Berkeley. Many other young quadriplegics saw an opportunity for education where there had been none before and also applied to Berkeley. A new social group was formed and they called themselves, "the rolling quads." Disability became a norm for the group. All of them were disabled to different extents. Wanting to get around the campus, go out with friends, and date, the young men developed new, innovative ways to achieve independence. They adapted wheelchairs that didn't keep breaking down. Disabled people in the community saw the new developments and asked for the inventions. The Center for Independent Living was, thus, formed. The purpose of the center was to support people with disabilities and to remove some of the barriers to independence that existed for people with disabilities. For example, when Berkeley city planned major street renovations, the group advocated curb cuts. Roberts eventually became the Director of the California Department of Rehabilitation, the same organization that believed that he was incapable of working. Roberts was a leader of the disabilities movement in the United States, helping many disabled people to live independent, productive, and happy lives. This case shows that social integration is not about changing the individual to match society. Social integration requires society to change to match the individual. Changing schools to make them accept children who are different, children with special medical needs, and youth who are LGBT, benefits everyone in the community.

CHAPTER 4

Diagnosis

For simplicity and clarity, adults prefer to label one party as the bully and the other person as the victim during bullying incidents. Bullying is rarely that clear. It can be very difficult to determine who is the bully and who is the victim. Bullies use several tactics to make the actions appear innocent or minor. He or she may smirk, laugh, or shrug off victim complaints. 'I was just joking' is a common response to bullying by bullies. Perpetrators rarely accept responsibility. The bully will try to claim that the actions were in response to some minor irritation by the victim. These tactics raise questions in the minds of onlookers. Potential defenders willingly go along with the bully's excuses because the bully is so confident and self-assured in side-stepping responsibility. Counter-aggression by the victim may further confuse bystanders. During interventions, bullies, who are good at manipulating adults, will make adults to believe that they are the victims. The first step in determining the victim and the bully is to determine who holds the power in the relationship. Carefully observing the underlying behaviors, attitudes, and reactions of each party can prevent bystanders from unknowingly supporting bullying.

SYMPTOMS OF VICTIMIZATION

Bullies select children who they think will be easy victims, children who won't or can't fight back, and children who others are not likely to help. Bullies are selective about potential targets. Possible gains must outweigh the energy and risks of the bullying. If the exploitation of a particular person requires too much energy, the bully will find another victim. The bully is not going to pick on a child who is bigger, likely to fight back, or has lots of friends. Easy victims are those who are small in stature, those who appear weak, those who are sensitive, cautious, or project some degree of vulnerability. Children who are quiet and dislike violence are perceived to be easy victims because the bully misperceives these characteristics as a lack of assertiveness. Some experts propose that children living in overprotective families make easy targets. The overprotectiveness of the family limits the child's ability to select good friends or resolve conflicts. These concepts of what makes a victim a victim are not intended to blame the victim. Every child has the right to live in a safe community, free of bullying. The factors are presented as a way to provide an insight as to who bullies are most likely to select as possible targets and which children may need greater protection.

Contrary to some beliefs, victims do not have traits that make them stand out, such as red hair, freckles, or glasses. However, children who are different may have trouble making friends, which would put them at risk of victimization. In schools, students at risk of victimization are those who have few friends, those who are new to a school, and those who are different. Children who have few friends are at higher risk because bullies know that they are easy targets, and no one is going to protect them. Likewise, children who are new to a school have not had the time to form strong relationships. Peers will not risk injury or attracting the bully's attention by protecting someone whom they do not have a connection with.

Victims characteristically display two very dissimilar reactions to bullying. The victim is either silent and withdrawn or provocative and angry. Passive victims are those who accept the abuse and do not fight back. They withdraw and isolate themselves. Few studies have investigated why victims respond in the way that they do. Passive victims may have views that violence is not the way to solve problems or they may have low self esteem, believing that they somehow deserve the abuse. Provocative victims respond to bullying with aggression. They fight back. Provocative victims tend to be irritating, fascinated by violence, easily provoked, impulsive, frequently in physical fights or verbal disputes, and disliked by others. Provocative victims are typically loners or hang out with peers who are also preoccupied with violence. Bystanders tend to find provocative victims irritating, which means that some adults will allow other students to bully the provocative victim. The adults may actively encourage the bullying by treating the child with disrespect in the classroom or they may passively encourage bullying by turning away and pretending not to see the attacks. Despite maltreatment by adults, provocative victims are optimistic about adult intervention. They assume that adults will get involved if they only know what is going on. Provocative victims will often report bullying to adults, over and over again, and despite a non-response, they maintain faith that adults will stop the bullying.

There are many physical and emotional signs that a child or youth is the victim of bullying. The symptoms vary based on the type of bullying, personal characteristics of the victim, and the length of victimization. Obvious signs of victimization are unexplained or poorly explained ripped clothing, cuts or bruises, missing personal belongings, such as electronic devices, jewelry, money, or expensive clothing. The loss of personal items may be because the bully and henchmen steal the items or the victim may have given items away in the hope of placating the attackers. If the bully takes lunch or lunch money, the child may be very hungry after school. Sudden changes in routine, such as taking a different route to or from school or a circuitous route between classrooms may be a sign of victimization. Visits to the nurses' office for somatoform disorders, disorders that do not have a clear physical reason—such as headaches, stomachaches, backaches, or other pains—are also a sign of bullying. Victims will use safe zones, such as the school nurses' office or a counselor's office, as a way to avoid high-risk areas or victims may have aches and pains brought on by emotional stress. Frequent trips to the doctor, dentist, or orthodontist, may provide ways to avoid bullying. More severe avoidance techniques are running away from home, skipping school, or switching to a private school. The National Association of School Psychologists estimated that an estimated 160,000 youth skip school every day due to bullying. Some victims have a sudden decrease in scholastic achievements because the bullying and avoiding the bully distract from learning. Some students who are bullied for being good students stop doing well in school as a way to avoid teasing. While there are many signs of victimization, sometimes the only sign is a general sense by the victim that he or she is being treated unfairly.

Depression is a major problem associated with bullying. Prolonged, relentless bullying can trigger depression. Signs of depression are changes in sleep habits, either too much or too little, feelings of worthlessness, feeling lousy about oneself, feeling isolated, hopeless, losing interest in fun activities, loss of appetite, or binge eating. Unexplained mood changes, such as sad, moody, anxious, or irritability, may be caused by bullying victimization. The combination of depression and bullying is particularly problematic because when victims are in a state of depression, they may blame themselves. Thoughts are chaotic. They may start to believe that they deserve the abuse. The depression impairs normal problem-solving abilities and the victims may stop making attempts to avoid or counter the abuse, which makes them easier targets. It is very difficult for victims suffering from depression to pull themselves out of the depression. Coming out of depression requires effort, focus, and determination—the very things that are destroyed by bullying and other abusive relationships. It is imperative that the depressed victim receive support, guidance, and assistance from outside professionals to cope with both the depression and the bullying.

The hopelessness, poor self esteem, and chaotic problem solving of depression can lead many victims to consider self-destructive responses. Fourteen percent of high school students report having seriously

The unrelenting trauma of bullying damages victims' emotional health. Victims feel useless and unwanted, and these feelings can lead to self-destructive behaviors. (AFH/ Shutterstock.com)

considered suicide in the past year. Eleven percent report making a plan and 6 percent report attempting suicide. This means that, in a normal-sized high school classroom, approximately two to three youth are considering suicide at any point in time. Warning signs for suicide are self-inflicted injuries, such as cutting or burning, giving away personal possessions, talking, writing, or joking about suicide, isolating oneself from others, actual suicide attempts, or engaging in dangerous behaviors that go beyond normal risk-taking. Depressed people may turn to self-destructive behaviors as a way to self-medicate against the depression. The depressed person may turn to alcohol, drugs, or self-mutilation as ways to deaden depression. This is unwise. Alcohol and some other commonly abused drugs are depressants and can aggravate the condition. Self-mutilation, such as cutting and burning initially release endorphins causing a temporary high. After the immediate sensation, these injuries increase the risk of infection and place more stress on the body, aggravating the depression. Friends and family members who are concerned should note that it is not uncommon for those considering suicide to show sudden signs of emotional improvement. The improvement may be an indication that the person has a plan for suicide. The belief that there may be an end to the suffering (through suicide) improves the mood. It is important not to misinterpret rapid changes in mood as positive. Anyone considering suicide should contact a medical or mental health professional or suicide hotline. Friends and family members can help those considering suicide by being alert for the telltale signs of depression and suicidal ideation and by responding in ways that acknowledge the problem and promote mental health.

Symptoms of Perpetration

In attempting to identify children who bully, it is important to recognize that bullies are not a distinct group of youth marked by antisocial behavior. Many children hit, push, or tease other youth. In fact, half of high school students report bullying another person (Josefson Institute, 2010). Bullies are normal, well-adjusted, and intelligent youth with healthy self-esteems (Salmivalli, 1998). Bullies are brothers, sisters, sons, daughters, nieces, nephews, cousins, and friends. Bullying is situation-specific, which means that bullies behave differently toward different people under different circumstances. A bully may be charming and likeable one minute and harsh and condescending the next minute. Some adults make the mistake of assuming that if a person is pro-social in one situation, he or she is always pro-social. Seeing bullies as people who are pro-social in some situations and antisocial in other situations helps identify perpetrators that would not be identified if bullies were considered a unique and isolated group of individuals. Placing bullies in a separate group of people demonizes some youth and inhibits school disciplinarians, coaches, and teachers from recognizing bullying by youth who are popular or socially advantaged. Understanding that normal youth can be bullies helps to identify all bullies, not just some. A second problem with placing bullies in a unique group is that adults are more likely to mete out harsher penalties for those who are different than those who are considered part of mainstream society. Schools have a history of not providing fair and consistent consequences. There are severe racial disparities in school discipline where youth with dark skin are more likely to be punished *and* to be punished more severely than children with light skin. In 1975, the rate of suspension for black students was three times the rate for white students (Children's Defense Fund, 1975). Not only were minority students more likely to be suspended, they received longer suspensions in comparison to other students. On the surface, these data may seem to suggest that black students violate rules more often than white students. This was not the case. Rates of rule violation do not vary significantly between minority and nonminority students (Skiba, Michael, Nardo, & Peterson, 2000). Researchers found that the differences in punishment were caused by how administrators interpreted school rules. Rules were interpreted more leniently for white students than for nonwhite students. Racial disparities continue even today in schools. School disciplinarians tend to use kinder, more empathetic methods to deal with infractions by children with light skin, wealth, or social connections. Recognizing that many children bully supports reasonable and consistent school discipline policies.

The main signs of a bully are a strong personality, positive attitudes toward violence, lack of empathy for others, and a strong sense of entitlement. Bullies show a need to dominate others from a very early age, some as early as preschool, and this trait continues into adulthood. The first sign that a child is moving toward becoming a bully is a failure to follow reasonable rules. The child who frequently violates boundaries, such as pushing other children while standing in line, taking toys from others without permission, or trying to get other children into trouble, is displaying feelings of entitlement that may put them at risk for bullying perpetration. This sense of entitlement is a sign of a bully. Bullies feel entitled to hurt others. The sense of entitlement also makes bullies believe that their actions will not be questioned or stopped by those in authority. Bullies feel that rules do not apply to them. Children who exhibit early signs of boundary violations and entitlement should be carefully monitored, and negative behaviors corrected with kind, positive strategies.

Two subtypes of bullies exist, sometimes classified as *hot* or *cold*. Bullies who are hot are short-tempered and reactionary. Provocative victims, victims who bully others, tend to be *hot*. They show anger, passion, fury, and other heated emotions. Their attacks are usually poorly planned because they are acting out of temper, without a great deal of forethought. Attacks are reactive, in response to a real or perceived threat. Once the attack is over, the hot bully will demonstrate true remorse, guilt, and regret. Hot bullies are upset by their own actions and pain inflicted on others. *Cold* bullies tend to be unemotional, callous, and lacking in empathy and guilt. They engage in thrill seeking behaviors with narcissistic tendencies. Cold bullies have trouble processing adverse stimuli, such as punishment, and are very sensitive to what they perceive as positive outcomes of the bullying, material or reward gains (Frick & Viding, 2009). Attacks are premeditated, well planned, and fearless. Callous, unemotional bullies are highly effective liars and show little remorse for their actions.

In performing violent acts, callous unemotional perpetrators go through a series of steps that allow them to overcome their own innate values against hurting other human beings. They convince themselves that the victim deserves the abuse and that they are the right person to mete out the abuse. Well-organized bullies may also go through steps to ensure minimal resistance to the attack by victims. Studies of men in battle reveal that human beings have a psychological aversion to killing or hurting other human beings. It is against man's inherent nature to hurt another member of the species unless the attack is due to competition for food during times of starvation or for mating purposes. This repugnance to hurting others is so deeply ingrained that armies developed ways to overcome this aversion. Boot camp, a brutal and punitive experience, desensitizes recruits to violence, making them believe that violence is a normal way of life. Weapon handling and firing are practiced over and over until the motions become automatic. The soldier loads and shoots without thinking. Soldiers are desensitized to killing others. Bullies also desensitize themselves to violence.

Possible ways that bullies are desensitized may be exposure to violence in the home, community, or media. Bullies are 4.4 times more likely to have been physically hurt by a family member than other youth (McKenna, Hawk, Mullen, & Hertz, 2009). Provocative victims are 5 times more likely to have been physically hurt by a family member (McKenna, Hawk, Mullen, & Hertz, 2009). Scientists are learning more and more about the impact of children's exposure to violence. It is believed that violence, such as that caused by harsh parenting or fighting in the home, alters the brain's nervous cells. Rather than developing normally, the brain focuses on survival. Early emotional trauma can cause permanent changes to the brain. Adults who were maltreated as children have a smaller hippocampus. The hippocampus is a part of the brain associated with memory and spatial navigation. As children, maltreated individuals show differences in the prefrontal cortex, an area of the brain important for decision making, emotional regulation, and social behavior. The brain exposed to chronic violence interprets any stimuli as a threat, even if it is not. The person may appear hypervigilant or belligerent. They misinterpret social cues, such as facial expressions and behaviors. They see neutral expressions or actions as aggressive when they are not. This means that when a person performs a benign or neutral action, the bully perceives it as a hostile action, a condition known as *hostile attribution bias*. This distorted thinking allows the bully to believe that an aggressive, punitive response is warranted. The bully rationalizes attacks, sometimes even believing that they have been the victim of attacks. Being alert for depersonalization and hostile attribution biases and correcting the distorted thought processes can help allay some bullying.

Normally, people are ashamed of hurting other people who are weak or helpless. Bullies protect their egos against this shame by imagining that the victim was not worthy of respect. The bully views the victim with disparagement or annoyance and this distorted thinking allows the bully to no longer view the victim as a human being with a right to safety or respect. This process is known as depersonalization and is common with violent offenders. Victims are blamed for their own victimization, such as when rape victims are blamed for their own sexual assault, victims of domestic violence are blamed for their injuries, or assault victims are blamed for being in the wrong place at the wrong time. When society believes that the victim did something to deserve the abuse, this absolves the perpetrator and bystanders of blame. The victim is hurt twice, once by the bully and again, by those who turn their back. Bullies lack empathy for others. They lack the ability to comprehend the hurt and pain that they cause. The depersonalization is compounded when school disciplinarians and teachers go along with the bully's distorted thinking. Adult complacency occurs more easily when the victim is unlikeable or irritating.

Once the bully has tricked his or her mind into believing that the attack is justifiable the next step is to perpetrate the violence. Risk factors for perpetrating violence are impulsiveness, history of experiencing harsh parenting, or having attitudes that accept violence. Children who are impulsive lack self-control. When upset, they cannot calm themselves down before they act or respond. In situations where an impulsive child is frustrated, the child may act aggressively. As children mature and learn to regulate their emotions, they develop better ways to respond to stressful situations and learn better self-control. When impulsiveness is combined with social power, a bully-prone personality develops. Inconsistent parenting also increases the potential for violence because parents who inconsistently apply rules do not give their children opportunities to learn rules. If the child gets in trouble sometimes and not others, it is hard for the child to learn how to behave normally in society. When parents use aggression to handle problems, the child learns to use aggression. Harsh punishment fosters resentment. The child resents the hurt of harsh discipline and resents the injustice of not knowing which behaviors are desirable and which behaviors are undesirable. With neglectful parenting, there is a lack of monitoring, which means that there are no limits set on the child's behavior. Neglect can also produce resentment because the child thinks that the parent does not care and acts out to gain attention. Although researchers know the risk factors for violence, this does not mean that every child with risk factors will become a bully. Children can learn to control impulsiveness. Practices such as counting from 1 to 10 before responding can minimize impulsive, aggressive reactions. If a child is irritated by another child at their locker, they can sing a song in their head while they make their way to a safe place, such as the guidance counselor's office or school nurse. There are things that children can do to overcome impulsiveness. A child who lives in an unstable family environment can find solace and stability in other places, such as at school, church, or grandparents' house. The daily routine of the school, the mentoring of a teacher, or the kindness of the school custodian can help to counterbalance a harsh home life. Even the child who has learned to act violently can be taught to channel that negative energy into a positive form, through drama, literature, painting, athletics, or music. Not every child who has the risk factors for violence will become violent.

CHAPTER 5

Health Consequences

Bullying victimization and perpetration have profound health, academic, and social effects on the victim, the bully, as well as bystanders. For victims, bullying is associated with feelings of loneliness, humiliation, insecurity, loss of self-esteem, and self-destructive behaviors. Victims fear attending school and may complain of psychosomatic problems or engage in truancy as ways to avoid attacks. School absences impact academic achievement, which can ultimately impact job and earning potential. Chronic bullying victimization can lead to poor mental health, substance abuse, depression, schizophrenia, and suicide. A small number of victims resort to suicide or school attacks. Bullies also suffer because they are more likely to progress to other antisocial behaviors, including smoking, drinking alcohol, vandalizing property, and dropping out of school. As adults, male bullies are more likely to get sent to jail and to have a higher number of convictions compared to males who do not bully. Incarceration, itself, impacts health, putting a person at risk for Hepatitis B, violence-related injuries, and mental health disorders. Finally, bystanders are impacted. Bystanders experience guilt and stress. Some bystanders report stress at the same level as people who have lost a home to fire or flood.

CONSEQUENCES OF VICTIMIZATION

Short and long term effects of bullying victimization vary greatly. Health consequences depend on the severity of the trauma, length of the exposure, how memories of the experience are integrated into the brain, strength of emotional supports, and many other variables. The health impact of bullying for victims, bullies, and bystanders can be divided into three categories: biological, psychological, and social. Biological refers to the physical state of the body. Biological effects can be measured through physical examination, X-rays, Computerized Axial Tomography (CAT) scans, Magnetic Resonance Imaging (MRI), and laboratory studies. Psychological effects are a little more difficult to measure because they are not as obvious. Trained counselors, psychologists, and psychiatrists have tools to measure depression, risk for suicide, and self-harming behaviors. Yet, stigmas against mental health services often prevent victims from seeking diagnosis and care. The victim's social damage is also fairly obvious. Bullying victimization makes one feel unwanted and alone. The impact of social exclusion is not easily measured, possibly due to the lack of recognition of the importance of social networks. In summary, victims of bullying can be impacted biologically, psychologically, and socially. Researchers are working to identify new ways to measure the extent of the damage caused by bullying.

The long-term biological and psychological impact of bullying victimization are highly interrelated. Biologically, the victims of physical bullying may suffer, with bruises, broken bones, lacerations, head, neck, or spine injuries. Some physical complaints may be due to the emotional nature of bullying. Physical ailments, such as increased sensitivity to pain, stomach upset, nausea, backaches, or stomachaches may be the result of psychological stress. Psychologically, victims suffer from feelings of low self-esteem, anxiety, insomnia, depression, suicidal thoughts, apathy, and problems with memory and concentration. Long-term effects can be post-traumatic stress disorder, eating disorders, self-harming behaviors, suicide, and other mental health problems, including schizophrenia. Bullying is a threat to the human body. The victim's body responds as it would to any other alarming event. Nerve cells send a message to the brain, instructing the brain to prepare for a possible threat. The brain kicks into high gear, collecting as much information as possible to determine whether the alarm is a threat or not. If the brain registers the event as a possible threat, the autonomic nervous system is activated. The autonomic nervous system regulates automatic reactions, those that the body does not consciously control. Reactions such as heart rate, breathing, blood pressure, skin temperature, and food digestion are all automatic. The brain does not have to consciously think about these processes. The autonomic nervous system prepares the body to either fight, flight, or freeze. The autonomic nervous system consists of the sympathetic nervous system and the parasympathetic nervous system. Normally, these two systems counterbalance each other to keep the body in homeostasis. Under threat, the sympathetic nervous system activates a stronger response. The sympathetic response diverts oxygen-carrying and nutrient-carrying blood cells to priority areas, such as the skeletal muscles. The skeletal muscles need oxygen and energy in order to run or fight. Simultaneously, the sympathetic nervous system releases the hormones and neurotransmitters, epinephrine and norepinephrine. The hormones provide a highly coordinated response, allowing different parts of the body to work together. Pupils widen to collect more information from the outside world, breathing passages expand to take in more oxygen, glucose is released from the liver as a quick source of energy for the brain and muscles, the heart beats stronger and faster to deliver oxygen, and blood is diverted away from the intestinal tract, a temporarily nonessential area.

The nervous system can respond to a stressor immediately. However, the results are not longlasting. Activating the body's nervous system is like turning a battery-powered radio on high. The radio can respond to the need for energy quickly but the battery will burn out if the high demand continues. Thus, the sympathetic system also triggers a process that can provide a more sustained response, the endocrine response. The endocrine system secretes hormones that stimulate other hormones to decrease insulin production so that the easily accessible glucose that is produced as a quick source of energy is not used up by nonessential areas, and to increase blood pressure to help the blood travel to needed areas. Fats and proteins are broken down for energy. Unfortunately, the body does not discriminate which proteins are broken down. The body disassembles almost any proteins, including antibodies that fight infection. Problems occur when the body is forced to handle prolonged, sustained threats, such as a victim would experience with chronic bullying. The body initially resists the stressor and then adapts to it by maintaining a constant state of arousal (Selye, 1956). This adaptation comes at a price. As the body breaks down fatty acids for energy, the risk of cardiovascular disease increases. The breakdown of proteins increases the risk of infection. High blood pressure increases the risk of kidney damage and heart attacks. Furthermore, because the body is depleted of energy, it is harder to fight infections. The individual is then at risk of attacks by viruses. Muscles waste away as the body becomes weaker and worn down. Chronic exposure to stress eventually leads to exhaustion. The person becomes physically and emotionally drained and, without proper care, may die.

Trauma theory provides health care workers with a framework to understand how individuals respond to stressors and how these responses influence future health and social behaviors. Examples of childhood traumatic events are chronic and severe bullying, fires, floods, physical or emotional assaults, sudden death of a loved one, or sexual abuse. Traumatic events are classified as simple or complex. Simple trauma is a single incident that occurs at a time when a person feels relatively safe. The feelings of safety provide a protective shield from the stressor. If the trauma occurs while the child feels loved and cherished by others, the child can cope with the trauma in healthy ways. Complex trauma is repeated, negative incidents that upset the victim's sense of safety or occur when the victim is already dealing with other, destabilizing traumas. While a victim may be able to handle simple trauma without any major health consequences, it is more difficult to deal with trauma combined with other adversities, such as an unstable family life, depression, or low self-esteem. Complex trauma causes toxic stress, a buildup of stress to the degree of exhaustion. In an attempt to deal with the stress, people will try to make sense of traumatic events. How the person responds, understands, and integrates the event into memory will influence other, later behaviors. The impact of traumatic events on the individual may not be apparent until months, years, or even decades after the incidents. In addition to the increased risk of infections, heart, and kidney diseases, individuals experiencing stress often turn to risky behaviors as a way to escape and forget about the trauma. Some of the health issues associated with traumatic events are cigarette smoking, alcohol and drug abuse, dangerous or thrill-seeking behaviors, weapon carrying, poor nutrition, or sexual risk taking. These unhealthy behaviors put people at greater risk of lung cancer, HIV/AIDS, sexually transmitted diseases, unwanted pregnancy, reproductive problems, heart disease, irritable bowel syndrome, and intentional and unintentional injuries.

The alienation and isolation of bullying can also have profound social effects. Victims are isolated and delegated to the lowest social status. The social alienation may be expressed as distrust of others, anger, or disengagement with school and social activities. The lack of trust may continue into adulthood as victims struggle to maintain partner relationships. *Betrayal trauma* is the term used to describe the anguish and personal violations experienced by victims when people who are supposed to protect the victim fail to do so (Freyd, 2008). Betrayal trauma is seen among families, friends, schools, workplaces, and community. It is not unusual for the trauma of betrayal to hurt more deeply and to have more lasting impact than the bullies' attacks. Holocaust survivor Elie Weisel said, "Let us remember; What hurts the victim most is not the cruelty of the oppressor but the silence of the bystander." Victims consider the betrayal as backstabbing, a violation of a trusted relationship or an unwritten social contract. Victims lose respect for the parent, adult, coach, or friend who fails to protect. The loss of respect can continue long after any physical injuries have healed. As adults, victims of bullying may have a severe distrust of educational institutions, teachers, coaches, or bosses.

Consequences of Perpetration

Bullies also suffer from health problems related to perpetration. Bullies show higher rates of drug abuse, defiance disorders, depression, psychiatric disorders, fighting, weapon carrying, early sexual activity, dating violence, and vandalism. These problems lead to other chronic problems.

Bullying can harm the bully. When youth are allowed to hurt others, they fail to learn normal social boundaries. With higher rates of fighting, weapon carrying, vandalism, and dating violence, many bullies eventually end up in jail. (Leah-Anne Thompson/Shutterstock.com)

Early sexual activity increases the risk of sexually transmitted diseases, such as HIV/AIDS and risk of teenage pregnancy, which impairs the ability to attain a college degree and to achieve a better lifestyle. Fighting and weapon carrying increase the risk of intentional and unintentional injuries. Vandalism and delinquency expose the youth to lifestyles that will introduce criminal behavior. Many bullies eventually end up in jail, often for multiple offenses. The presence of defiance disorders among bullies may be a basic personality trait or the result of their experiences with bullying. The normal, healthy child may push the limits of behavior because this allows the child to enjoy new experiences and to learn about the social and physical environment. With bullying, adults and teachers who are reluctant to stop or control antisocial behaviors, are unintentionally teaching the child that social boundaries are not important. The bully fails to learn normal limits of social behavior. This means that bullies will continue to push the limits until they cross lines and get into criminal activity. While most studies on the consequences of bullying perpetration show higher rates of defiance disorders, it is important to note that some bullies enjoy a very high social prestige and may enter adulthood without major health consequences.

Consequences of Combined Victimization and Perpetration

Provocative victims, victims who counter bullying with aggression, pose special health concerns because they have poorer mental health than bullies or victims. Provocative victims are both the bully and the victim. Thus, they are at risk of the health consequences of both groups. Provocative victims have higher rates of binge drinking, marijuana use, weapon carrying, truancy, and depression. Provocative victims tend to have fewer friends than other victims and are rated lower on social scales than passive victims. This extremely low level of social support means that provocative victims are often forced to handle the stress of bullying on their own, without appropriate assistance from others. Higher stress levels will increase the rates of chronic diseases, such as heart disease, some cancers, and self-inflicted injuries.

Consequences of Witnessing Bullying

Studies of bystanders show that bullying is also detrimental to witnesses. Most bystanders do not like watching another person being hurt and want to help the victim but do not know how. This internal conflict causes guilt, fear, stress, hyper vigilance, and emotional exhaustion. Some bystanders fear that if they intervene to stop the attack, they may become the next target. The stress experienced by bystanders is measured by heart rate and skin conductance. When researchers asked victims and witnesses of bullying to recall past incidents, they found very similar results. As victims of bullying described past incidents, their heart rate increased 24 percent and the skin conductance increased by 81 percent. As bystanders described past incidents of watching others being bullied, their heart rate increased 21 percent and skin conductance increased 81 percent (Janson & Hazler, 2004). Even more surprisingly, the level of emotional distress of bystanders was consistent with people experiencing serious life events, such as civil war, terrorism, rape, floods, fire, and tornadoes (Janson & Hazler, 2004). The actual impact of the exposure is based on the duration of the abuse exposure, resiliency, and perceived vulnerability of the bystander. Prolonged exposure may trigger post-traumatic stress disorder. Bullying impairs the spiritual, emotional, and social health of bystanders. Because bullying has such severe effects on bystanders, some experts advocate referring to bystanders as co-victims.

In severe cases of bullying, there may be legal consequences for adult bystanders who fail to act. People who work with children are *mandated reporters,* which means they are required by law to report observed or suspected cases of child maltreatment or neglect to child welfare authorities.

Doctors, nurses, teachers, counselors, coaches, and other professionals working with children, disabled people, or vulnerable populations are trained in how to recognize the symptoms of abuse, and how and where to file a report. Mandated reporters are required to report how they gained the information, what they observed, details of the incident, such as time, place, alleged perpetrator, and the name, agency, position, and contact number of the mandated reporter. While mandated reporters are not legally obligated to notify parents or guardians that they have filed a report, it may be advantageous. The parent or guardian may eventually find out who filed the report and an honest and full disclosure will help the parent understand the need for reporting. In some cases, mandated reporting can be beneficial in that the family may be given access to services that they would not have had if the report were not filed. There are severe criminal and civil consequences for failing to report or filing a false report. Minimally, a professional can be fired for failing to report bullying that rises to the level of child maltreatment.

Financial Consequences to Schools and Communities

The financial consequences of bullying are immense. Financial expenses due to bullying include medical treatment, mental health care, lost productivity and academic achievement, disability, lower quality of life, premature death, school security, and legal costs (Pinheiro, 2006). Bullying causes substantial economic losses to workplaces, schools, and communities. In addition to direct and indirect costs, there is the damage to reputation due to undesirable media attention. The loss of good public relations may take years or even decades to recover. Overall, the estimated cost of youth violence in the United States is $158 billion each year (Pereznieto, Harper, Clench, & Coarasa, 2010). School violence, including bullying, is estimated to cost between $14.4 billion and $40.3 billion, representing 0.1 to 0.3 percent of the Gross Domestic Product, the total value of goods and services produced by the United States (Pereznieto, Harper, Clench, & Coarasa, 2010).

For a typical high school serving 1,000 students, the estimated costs of bullying are $2.3 million per year (Phillips, n.d.). The first factor accounting for bullying costs is truancy. An estimated 8 percent of middle school students skip school due to fears for personal safety (Perkins, Perkins, & Craig, 2009). This modestly translates to a cost of $21,600 per year (Phillips, n.d.). The estimated cost of suspensions is $290 for a total cost of $17,400 per year (Phillips, n.d.). With an expulsion rate of 2 percent, the annual cost of expulsion is $75,400 (Phillips, n.d.). Dropping out of school costs an estimated $2.16 million (Phillips, n.d.). Placement in an alternative school is estimated at $25,000 per year (Phillips, n.d.). Vandalism, the final cost, arises out of a lack of connection to the school. Vandalism costs are estimated at $15,200 (Phillips, n.d.). This calculation excludes medical treatment in nurses' offices, emergency rooms, legal fees, and administrative costs for cases that do not result in suspensions and exclusions. The majority of these costs are paid for by taxpayers.

CHAPTER 6

Causes of Bullying

For many health problems, it is impossible to name only one, specific cause. Heart disease, for instance, is caused by a combination of hereditary factors, physical inactivity, and poor nutrition. Car crashes are caused by alcohol and drugs, poor or inexperienced driving skills, and bad road conditions. Certain factors may increase or decrease the risk of a health problem. Researchers identify links between risk factors and diseases through multiple research studies. The studies are aimed at proving *causality*. In order to say with certainty that a particular factor causes a particular disease, the factor must meet the *conditions of causality*. Conditions of causality are a set of conditions that suggest the relationship between a specific factor and a health outcome. The conditions of causality are: time sequence between cause and effect, biological credibility, consistency with other investigations, dose–response relationship, and any relationship that cannot be explained by a third factor (Hennekens & Buring, 1987). The condition of appropriate time sequence requires that the causal factor must precede the outcome. This seems pretty straightforward. Cigarette smoking must come before lung cancer in order to say that smoking probably caused the cancer. Time sequence becomes unclear when there is a long time span between the cause and the effect. The problems with exposure to violence as a child may not be realized for decades after the exposure. The condition of biological credibility means that the current knowledge of human anatomy and physiology should support causality. There is biological plausibility to the idea that exposure to violence increases the risk of perpetration, in that stress increases cortisol levels, which can impact normal neurological development which can put someone at risk for acting aggressively. The condition of consistency with other investigations means that multiple investigations that study the problem in a variety of ways have come up with similar conclusions. Studies that look back in time, asking perpetrators about past history of exposure; studies that look forward in time, determining differences between children exposed to violence and those not exposed to violence; and studies in the community must show consistent results for experts to draw conclusions about the role of exposure in causing increased violence. The condition of a dose–response relationship means that there is a relationship between the dose and the response, where the greater the dose of the risk factor, the greater the response. People who smoke a full pack of cigarettes a day have a higher dose of carcinogens and will have a greater risk of cancer. The same should be true for violence. Greater exposure to violence should increase the risk of violence. The final condition of causality is that the outcome cannot be explained by a third factor or a moderating variable. This is where researchers struggle. It is very difficult to rule out all other causes. With childhood exposure to domestic violence, role modeling is a third variable. Girls exposed to violence against their mothers are at greater risk of victimization as they enter into their own intimate relationships. Males exposed to violence against their mothers are at greater risk for perpetration. Differences appear to be based on which parent the child takes on as a role model. If females adapt their father as a role model, they are likely to take on the aggressor role. It takes time, effort, and detailed investigations in order to say that a specific factor causes a specific condition. In bullying, where there are so many moderating variables—the reaction of the victim, support of the bully, environmental opportunities, and so on—it is difficult to point with certainty the exact causes of bullying. This is why some experts prefer to skip over discussing causal factors.

Like causality, health behavior—why people act in the way that they do with respect to health—is very complicated. Many factors merge together to cause a behavior. Models and theories propose ways to understand health behaviors, issues, and diseases. Theories provide a comprehensive, systematic way to view the problem, avoiding a hit or miss approach. Theories are developed from research and general consensus of experts in the field. In bullying, theories provide suggestions of why people bully, why bystanders act the way that they do, why some victims fight back and others do not, and why bullying is more common in some institutions than in others. For example, Social Learning Theory is a theory that describes how people learn behaviors such as aggression. The model presents many complex factors that may not be considered if a person was not using a model. The model includes factors such as watching others act violently, belief in one's ability to perform the observed behavior, and enforcers of the behavior. Theories combined with practice provide strong, plausible explanations of why people behave the way they do. However, merely understanding the reasons behind the behavior is not enough. In order to stop the problem, theories must be translated into practice. Practice refers to the action of improving health. In medicine, practice refers to medical treatments, radiology, physical therapy, speech therapy, occupational therapy, surgical procedures, or other proven and accepted treatments in the field. Practice develops from experience, skill, and communication of what treatments work and what treatments do not work to alleviate the problem. Best practices or evidence-based practices are those practices which have been proven to work in research. Combining valid theories and best practices provides the most successful treatments.

Through research, scientists have identified multiple biological, social, and developmental factors that predispose a person to violent behavior. At the individual level, low IQ, antisocial beliefs, exposure to violence and conflict in the family, history of victimization, involvement with drugs, alcohol, or tobacco, attention deficits, emotional problems, learning disorders, hyperactivity, and impaired ability to process information increases risk of violent perpetration (U.S. Department of Health and Human Services, 2001). Risk factors at the family level are harsh, negligent, or overbearing disciplinary practices, poor emotional attachments between parent and child, low income and educational level, dysfunctional communication and behaviors, and parental substance abuse or criminality (USDHHS, 2001). Peer and social factors that promote violence are association with antisocial peers, poor academic performance, and feeling little connection to the school community (USDHHS, 2001). Risk factors in communities are lack of jobs and resources, crowded living conditions, disorganized community structure, and transient populations with little financial or emotional investment in the neighborhood (USDHHS, 2001). Most of the risk factors for violence translate directly into bullying perpetration. Bullies show greater support for aggressive behaviors, are not well connected to their school, and believe that peers are untrustworthy (Williams & Guerra, 2007). In most cases, there is not one specific factor that causes a person to bully another. Violence-related behaviors result from multiple factors working in combination. Some factors increase the risk of perpetration while others decrease the risk. Thus, it is not one specific factor that causes bullying, but the interrelationship of multiple factors working together. There are several theories of why people bully others. No single theory can explain the causes of all violence-related behavior. This section introduces the main theories of why people bully, starting with the individual and moving on to the larger social and cultural environment. In reviewing these theories, it is important to consider how each theory can be translated into practice and what each theory suggests in terms of how to stop bullying.

Biological

Biologically, aggressive behaviors have been linked to brain malfunction, complications during pregnancy, genetics, neurotransmitters, hormones, and abnormal brain development (Moeller, 2001). Theories about the biology of aggression initially developed from opportunistic knowledge, observations of behavioral changes that existed among people suffering from stroke, traumatic brain injury, epilepsy, neurological, or genetic disorders (Pontegal, Stemmler, & Spielberger, 2010). When a specific region of the brain is injured, the affected person shows deficiencies that reveal information about how that area of the brain functions. Feelings of anger increase approximately 32 percent within the first 3–12 months after a stroke (Kim, Choi, Kwon, & Seo, 2002). Approximately one-third of people with dementia exhibit signs of agitation and aggressiveness that were not apparent before the onset of dementia (Lyketsos, Lopez, Jones, Fitzpatrick, Breitner, & DeKosky, 2002). Deficiencies help scientists to understand which areas of the brain control movement, cognition, and behavior. If the victim of the disorder shows increased tendencies toward violence, scientists have an opportunity to learn about that specific area of the brain. Scientists are still learning about the different areas of the brain and how each area works alongside other areas.

Traumatic brain injury (TBI) is a jolt or blow to the body or head that is severe enough to cause an injury to the brain. Brain injuries range from mild, where the person suffers temporary confusion and disorientation, to severe, where the person suffers from unconsciousness and amnesia. An estimated 1.7 million TBIs occur every year in the United States (Faul, Xu, Wald, & Coronado, 2010). The most common causes of TBI are falls, motor vehicle crashes, sports, and assaults (Faul, Xu, Wald, & Coronado, 2010). High-risk groups for TBI are young children and the elderly. Depending on the severity of the injury, the person suffering from TBI may experience changes in thinking, senses, language, and emotions. Impaired reasoning and emotions can increase the risk of violence-related behaviors. People suffering from moderate to severe TBI may show changes in personality after the injury. Some of the changes observed include inappropriate social behaviors, acting out, and aggression. People with damage to the frontal lobe experience changes in emotional regulation and problem-solving abilities. Frontal lobe damage produces personality changes, where the person becomes less spontaneous, engages in more risky behaviors, and disregards rules (Blumer & Benson, 1975). There are differences in personality changes, depending on which side of the frontal lobe is damaged. Damage to the right frontal lobe is associated with psychopathic tendencies whereas damage to the left frontal lobe may exhibit as depression (Blumer & Benson, 1975). A person with damage to the frontal lobe shows an overreaction to a trigger. Anger is directed at the cause of the problem. In contrast, a person with damage to the temporal lobe can also exhibit anger, but the anger is poorly focused. The adverse outcomes of TBI can be limited by immediate medical treatment after the injury, rest, avoiding re-injury while the brain is healing from the injury, and occupational therapy to help the person deal with loss of memory or other changes in the brain function. TBI can be prevented through wearing seatbelts; avoiding driving under the influence of drugs or alcohol; wearing helmets during biking, skateboarding, baseball or snowboarding; maintaining a soft surface under playground equipment; and removing tripping or falling hazards in the home and work environments.

Behavioral genetics is a relatively new field that investigates how much of a particular behavior is due to genetics and how much is due to environmental influence. Among many other questions, behavioral genetics seeks to answer whether aggressive behaviors, such as bullying, are due to genetics, the environment, or both. Known as the nature vs. nurture controversy, experts previously debated whether a trait was inherited or triggered by the environment. The current line of thought is that characteristics may fall into three categories: those which are purely due to genetics, those which are purely due to the environment, and those which are due to both genetics and the environment. It is believed that some people are born with a gene that predisposes them to certain behaviors. These behaviors are only exhibited if the person is exposed to triggers in the environment. Triggers for violence-related behavior may be exposure to pollutants, violence in the home or community, or modeling by parents or other adults. For example, males are typically considered more violent. Violence-related gender differences may be due to genetics, hormonal influences, role socialization, or other factors (Reiss & Roth, 1993). Existing genetic influences are strengthened or diminished based on environmental or social factors.

Behavioral geneticists use several methods to determine how much of a trait is genetic and how much is environmental. Studies of identical and fraternal twins or children adopted soon after birth are used to determine the strength of genetic influence. Twin studies suggest that 47 percent of the variation in hostility is due to genetics (Coccaro, Bergeman, Kavoussi, & Seroczynski, 1997). Genetics may also act indirectly to produce violence-related behaviors. Defects in the genes that code the enzymes monoamine oxidase (MAOA) and tryptophan hydroxylase (TPH) appear to increase tendencies toward violence (Brunner, Nelen,

Breakefield, Ropers, & van Oost, 1993; Manuck, Flory, Ferrell, Dent, Mann, & Muldoon, 1999). MAOA breaks down neurotransmitters after usage. MAOA deficiencies are associated with impulsiveness and criminal behavior. TPH helps to synthesize serotonin, a neurotransmitter that influences the mood. Overall, scientists believe that genetics has a moderate influence on aggressive tendencies. This influence should be interpreted with caution. When scientists attempted to breed highly aggressive strains of mice, they found that levels of aggressiveness returned to normal levels within several generations of regular breeding (Nelson, 2006).

Alcohol and other drugs also have a direct effect on human physiology and an indirect effect on violent behavior. Approximately one-third of homicides and suicides are associated with alcohol (Karch, Dahlberg, & Patel, 2010). Sixty percent of violent death victims with alcohol in their system had a blood alcohol concentration above the legal driving limit (Karch, Dahlberg, & Patel, 2010). Thirty-seven percent of state prisoners and 21 percent of federal prisoners serving time for a violent crime were under the influence of alcohol at the time of the crime (Bureau of Justice Statistics, 2010). Alcohol is a depressant drug that impairs judgment, increases self confidence, reduces attention span, and increases risk taking, at lower doses. Alcohol reduces social inhibition, which means that people under the influence act in ways that they would not normally act, including fighting, making violent threats, or verbally abusing others. Alcohol has a direct effect on violent behavior in that it allows people to act more aggressively. Studies have shown that heterosexual intimate partner violence is eight times higher on days when the man consumes alcohol, while the rate of more severe attacks is increased 11 times (O'Farrell, Fals-Stewart, Murphy, & Murphy, 2003). Alcohol has an indirect influence on bullying in that it affects the immediate environment, including interpersonal relationships. With respect to bullying, there is a further link between alcohol abuse and bullying as children of alcoholic parents are at greater risk of bullying perpetration and victimization. The association may be due to genetics, the fact that alcohol impairs bonding between parent and child, or a combination of both factors.

Evidence of biological causes of violence raises important questions for the treatment and prevention of violence-related disorders. If a behavioral disorder, such as aggressiveness, is due to atypical genetics, should the person be forced to undergo gene therapy? Does the defense of "my genes made me do it" provide a legitimate excuse for criminals facing prosecution? Will carriers of certain disorders be discouraged from having offspring? Who will determine which gene types are considered typical and which are atypical, and in need of treatment? There is still much research to be done and questions to be answered in the field of behavioral genetics.

Frustration–Aggression

Early psychologists believed that violence was cathartic, people who acted violently were releasing built-up frustration. A group of researchers from Yale University proposed a link between frustration and aggression, which supposed that aggression resulted when people were intentionally blocked from reaching a desired goal. Frustration is a negative emotion, characterized by feelings of dissatisfaction and ineffectiveness. People who are frustrated may feel deceived and discouraged. Aggression is a forceful action marked by hostility or destructiveness. When people were unable to achieve an expected goal, they became frustrated and this frustration, under certain circumstances, was expressed as aggression (Dollard, Doob, Miller, Mowrer, & Sears, 1939). The individual who was perceived as being responsible for the frustration became the target of hostility. The researchers acknowledged that aggression did not always result from frustrated goals. Certain conditions are necessary, such as the fact that the person must want and expect the goal. If the person seeking the goal does not expect the goal, then the person might not feel frustrated. If the person does not really care whether the goal is attained, then the person may not feel frustrated at all. If the person achieves part of the goal and is partially satisfied, then the person may not feel frustrated. The degree of interference and intentionality of the interference can also temper the aggressiveness. If the interference is minimal and does not actually interfere with the goal or only mildly delays goal achievement, the person may not become aggressive. If the interference is unintentional, the person may not become aggressive. In order for an aggressive response to occur, the aggressor must be strong and confident enough to express the aggression. If the person is timid and fearful, the aggression may be repressed. Dollard et al. also noted the concept of residual aggression, where the potential aggressor is able to overcome each obstacle but the feelings of discouragement and frustration add up to eventually produce breaking point. While the source of the obstacles is the most obvious target for aggression, there are some cases where the aggressor realizes that it is unwise to attack the person doing the blocking. The aggressor may fear discipline, loss of job, or other social consequences. In these cases, the aggression may be played out on a third party.

In terms of bullying, the bully or provocative victim is the aggressor. The bully who acts out of frustration–aggression is reacting to a situation, person, or event. Someone, or something, is blocking the bully from desired goals and the victim is either perceived as the source of the impediment or as an acceptable substitute for the frustration/aggression. The frustrated–aggressive bully is angry and impulsive, driven by heated emotions. The reaction is overly aggressive to what the situation warrants. The bully may be frustrated by school, unable to perform as well as desired. If the victim is studious, performing well in school, the bully will perceive the victim as competition and the source of frustration. The victim will become the target of aggression. Alternatively, the bully may feel that the teacher is the source of the frustration. However, attacking the teacher would be counterproductive to achieving the goal and could result in disciplinary action. The victim serves as an alternative target. In some cases, the frustration may be unconscious—the bully may be experiencing pent-up frustration due to a lack of physical activity during the school day, frustrations with finding potential dating partners, frustrations from having to sit in school and follow rules all day, a provocative victim who has been pushed to the breaking point, or a child dealing with an unstable family life. Aggression is perceived as a way to gain control. Bullying rooted in frustration-aggression is typically thoughtless. The perpetrator usually does not have a well-conceived plan beyond the bullying. After the abuse, the hostile bully may feel sad, guilty, depressed, or suicidal. Major criticisms of the hypothesis are that the researchers generalized their theory to all experiences with frustration and that the theory was developed based on empirical observations, not scientific studies. Not everyone who is frustrated will act aggressively (Berkowitz, 1993). There are cognitive and emotional mediators that seem to block the development of aggression. In some instances, blocked goals produce positive outcomes, such as creative problem solving, new discoveries, and alternative plans.

Narcissistic Personality

While frustration–aggression theory explains some of the instances of hot bullying, narcissistic personality disorder explains some cases of cold bullying. Narcissism is a personality trait characterized by feelings of superiority that are not well grounded in reality. The narcissist is condescending and arrogant, openly expressing jealousy and contempt for others. The narcissist brags about exaggerated achievements and fantasizes of power and success. Because their stories of power and triumph are entertaining and attractive, narcissists have no trouble attracting supporters. Unfortunately, they are so wrapped up in their own self-admiration that they fail to recognize other people's feelings or needs. They devalue or minimize their friend's achievements in order to raise themselves up. This insensitivity or lack of empathy for others puts narcissists at high risk of bullying perpetration. Narcissists need constant admiration. They prefer to surround themselves with people who provide constant, positive attention.

People who refuse to feed the narcissist's ego are shunned or become the target of abuse. It is difficult for the narcissist to maintain long-term relationships. As would-be supporters get to know the narcissist, the façade of superiority crumbles, and personal weaknesses are revealed. The narcissist is highly sensitive to criticism and becomes very defensive and aggressive. Narcissists will attack those who dare to question or disagree. Thus, narcissists are at risk of abusing anyone because putting others down makes narcissists feel better about themselves and they are also particularly at risk of attacking people who disagree or mildly criticize them.

Narcissism is thought to develop from maladaptive social development. All children exhibit some degree of egocentric or narcissist behavior. Infants and toddlers are not able to comprehend a world beyond their immediate environment. As children mature, they meet other children with needs. The sense of egocentrism gradually deteriorates. Children develop empathy and understanding for others. Children who are neglected, abused, or have overindulgent parents have difficulty learning empathy. They continue to age, but with an immature ego. The superiority, lack of empathy for others, and sense of personal entitlement promotes bullying perpetration. Narcissistic bullies are difficult to treat because they will not admit that they have a problem. They will always point to the victim as the source of the problem.

Adolescent Development

Adolescence is a time of rapid hormonal change and physical and emotional growth. Teenagers struggle with changes in their body, finding a role in society, and achieving independence. Adolescents are a walking contradiction. They have the body of an adult but the brain of a child. The frontal lobe, the part of the brain that guides judgment and decision-making skills, is not fully developed until the mid-twenties. The last part of the human brain to develop is the prefrontal cortex. The prefrontal cortex guides reflection, consideration of possible solutions, and critical problem-solving. Lacking a fully functioning prefrontal cortex, teenagers must rely on other areas of the brain to help make decisions. Adolescents use the amygdala, a portion of the brain that regulates emotional reactions. This means that the teenager depends on gut reactions to make decisions. The lack of prefrontal cortex function leads youth to misinterpret facial expressions. They are not able to read a person's emotions and easily misinterpret other people's reactions to events, behaviors, and circumstances. The inability to read nonverbal body language is particularly relevant to bullies. Teenaged bullies, without a fully formed brain, may be incapable of interpreting and understanding victim responses. Some bullies may be unable to see and understand the pain which they inflict.

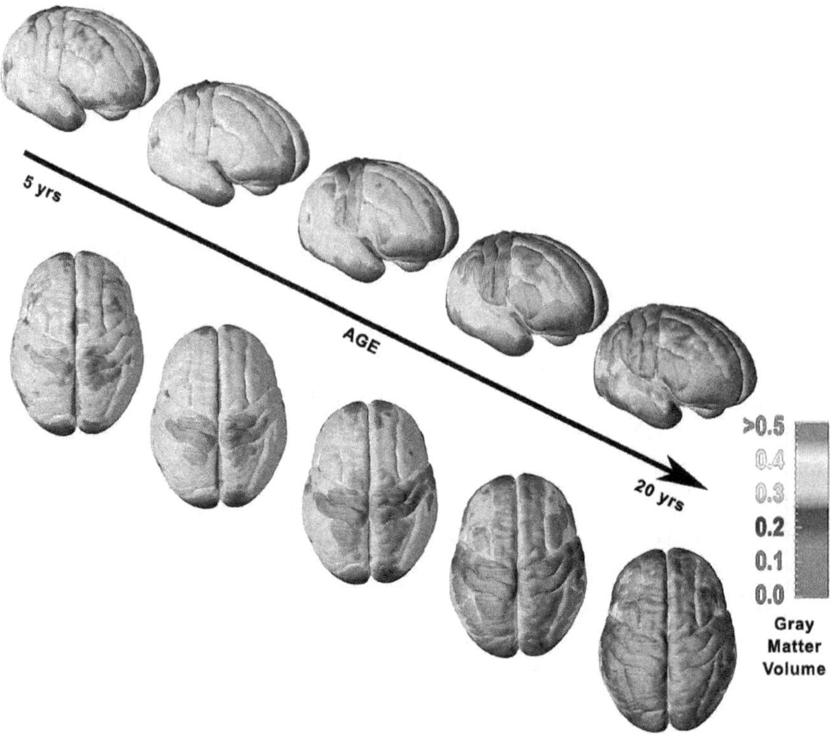

Brain scans show that the human brain continues to develop well into the mid-twenties. The last parts of the brain to form are the areas that govern judgment and decision making. [Images courtesy of Dr. Paul Thompson, UCLA Medical Center]

Socially, adolescents are curious and like to test new behaviors. This pilot-testing allows them to try different roles in order to find one which feels comfortable. The Pathways Models are concepts which help to understand emerging adolescent identities (Moffitt, 1993). Pathways models are envisioned as different paths or roles that adolescents try out that lead to adult behaviors. Loeber's Pathways Model describes three violence-related pathways: *authority conflict, overt violence-related behavior,* and *covert violence-related behavior* (Loeber & Stouthamer-Loeber, 1998). The authority conflict pathway is characterized by stubbornness, defiance, truancy, and running away, or staying out late, prior to the age of 12. The overt violence-related pathway is characterized by minor aggression, such as bullying, which progresses to the more violent behaviors of physical fighting, rape, or assault. The covert violence-related pathway starts with shoplifting or lying and progresses to property damage, fraud, burglary, or serious theft. As youth stay on a particular pathway, there is an opportunity to meet others on the pathway and to refine skills and behaviors into adult violence.

There are two identified time points for entry to violent pathways: before puberty and during adolescence (Moffitt, 1993). These time periods, late elementary school to early middle school, and high school to early college, trade school or career, are high-risk times for youth to experiment with violence. Not all youth who engage in violence are destined to become criminals. Some youth simply grow out of the behaviors and are no longer attracted to them (Eron, Gentry, & Schlegel, 1994). Peer influence and fear of social ostracism also provide limits. The desire for individualism is overruled by the need to be part of a social group and being part of a group requires conformity. Currently, the Pathways Model is limited in that the researchers only studied males. Less is known about violence-related behavior among females. Additionally, criminal behaviors are defined by society. A behavior construed as criminal in one set of circumstances may be acceptable under another set. For example, in some states, concealing merchandise is shoplifting. This means that bagging groceries at the time of purchase technically meets the definition of shoplifting. Yet, not too many people are arrested for bagging their own groceries.

The Pathways Model applies to several different aspects of bullying. The model supposes that undesirable adolescent behaviors are self-limiting. This means that bullies will not always be bullies. With the correct social and emotional support, some bullies will outgrow bullying. The act of bullying requires social conformity. It is very easy for the bully to pull peers into the aggressive and harmful behaviors of attacking the victim because peers are seeking new behaviors to test. The group process overrules individual thought. Henchmen act in ways that they would never have adopted if on their own. The bully can anticipate that the victim, henchmen, bystanders, and adults will respond in expected ways. If any of these parties fails to act in the way that the bully expects, the entire bullying process is disrupted. Several evidence-based programs work by disrupting the group process, encouraging youth to reframe their perspective and to think for themselves. Benefits of the model are recognition that the normal adolescent is balancing two unique and disparate goals, individualism and social conformity, and bullying prevention experts can use these goals to disrupt attitudes and behaviors that support bullying.

Violence as a Learned Behavior

Many researchers have studied how or why people adopt violent tendencies. An early sociological researcher, Edwin Sutherland (1939) proposed that infants are not born with antisocial tendencies. People learn delinquent behaviors when they associate with people who are already engaged in such behaviors. When the number and degree of interactions with active offenders outnumbers the degree of interactions with law-abiding citizens, the individual is at risk of adopting antisocial behaviors. The theory explains why programs that bring groups of antisocial youth together for treatment do not work. The groups simply become a training ground for more severe antisocial behavior. Sutherland's Differential Association Theory upset previous ideas that proposed that criminality was genetic or due to brain disease. The theory formed the foundation for later research into violence as a social and learned behavior, related to geographic, economic, and political influences.

Social Cognitive Theory (SCT) is a theory that describes how people learn social and health behaviors (Bandura, 1986). The theory proposes that children learn violence by watching other people engage in violence. Children who witness threats, hitting, slapping, punching, beating, or attacking with a weapon are likely to develop violence-related behavior (Fitzpatrick & Boldizar, 1993). Exposure to violence influences the viewer by (1) introducing and modeling behaviors that the observer may not have thought of alone; (2) immunizing the observer against instincts that reject violence; and (3) presenting violence as a normal aspect of life, when it is not (Shapiro et al., 1998). SCT has been supported by many research studies. Among adolescent males, exposure to violence accounts for 50 percent of the variation in violent behaviors and among adolescent females, exposure accounts for 42 percent of the variation in violent behaviors (Song, Singer, & Anglin, 1998). Youth who bully others witness violence in the home at a rate of three times more than other children. Bully victims report witnessing violence at home four times the rate of other youth (McKenna, Hawk, Mullen, & Hertz, 2009). Exposure to violence not only influences the child who is observing, but also other children, as they also mimic the undesirable behaviors. Exposure to violence is associated with increased willingness to use aggression to solve problems, decreased perception of the risk of participating in dangerous behaviors, unhappiness, antisocial behavior, poor school grades, and alcohol use (Schwab-Stone et al., 1995).

SCT proposes specific factors that support learning, including learning how to bully. At the heart of SCT is the concept of *reciprocal determinism,* where individuals influence the environment and the environment influences individuals. Reciprocal determinism applies to bullying in that, when bullying occurs in school, observers not only learn how to bully but also start to believe that bullying is normal and accepted as part of the school environment. Once bullying starts in a school or workplace, the behavior becomes endemic (Harvey, Treadway, & Heames, 2007; Strandmark & Hallberg, 2007). Endemic means that the problem is native to the area. It is deeply engrained in the environment. The basic building blocks of SCT are observational learning, situations, self-efficacy, expectations, expectancies, and reinforcements. When all of these components or constructs are in the right combination, individuals acquire the behavior more easily. Observational learning is the idea that people learn by watching other people. Younger children learn by watching older children. New children learn by watching children who are already accustomed to a particular school or community. Situations endorse the specific behaviors. If there are multiple opportunities to observe the behavior or the situation supports learning the behavior, the child is more apt to learn the behavior. If the child sees other children bullying and getting away with it, the observer may attempt to bully. If the child sees other children bullying and staff intervene to stop the attack, the observer is less likely to attempt bullying. Self-efficacy is the confidence that observers have in their ability to perform the behavior. Hitting, kicking, and pushing are not difficult behaviors to enact. It would be easy for a child to mimic these behaviors. Bullying, in itself, requires an imbalance of power. So, true bullying is harder to enact than pseudo bullying behaviors, behaviors that mimic bullying without the underlying abuse of power. Observers are more likely to copy the behavior if they believe the behavior has valuable benefits. The belief that the behavior has benefits is known as expectations. The belief that the benefits have value is expectancies. Bullying offers several benefits (*expectations* and *expectancies*). Bullies may use bullying as a way to compete for grades, scholarships, college placements, dating partners, or jobs (Strandmark & Hallberg, 2007; Twemlow & Sacco, 2007). The advantages are even more valuable if the bully does not have the academic or technical skills to engage in fair competition. The last component of SCT is reinforcement. Reinforcements are rewards that promote the behavior (Baranowski, Perry, & Parcel, 1997). Internal reinforcers may be that the bully feels more powerful and in control when bullying or feels a personal satisfaction. External reinforcers may be the instrumental gains, such as lunch money or personal possessions of the victim, or may be the perceived admiration from henchmen and bystanders. When all of these components come together in ways that support and reinforce bullying, the observing child is more likely to attempt bullying. As more and more children attempt and practice bullying, bullying becomes a way of life within the organization or community.

Moral Development

Some bullying may be due to moral development whereby the bully, the victim, bystanders and authorities are at incongruent levels of moral development. Bullying involves multiple, simultaneously occurring moral judgments. The first moral judgment is in how the bully rationalizes the attacks. The second moral judgment is made by the victim in determining how to respond. The third moral judgment is made by the immediate bystanders in determining whether they should intervene or how to intervene. The fourth moral judgment is made by those in positions of authority in determining how to handle incidents, the bully, the victim, and the bystanders.

Lawrence Kohlberg (1969) identified six stages of moral judgment. The stages differ, not by the morality of the final action, but by how the decision for action is made, the underlying thought processes of the thinker. For example, people who obey rules because they fear punishment are at a different level than people who obey rules because an inner moral conscience dictates that they act a certain way. People can advance through the stages, stay at a particular stage, or apply different levels of thinking to different situations. Very few people achieve the highest level of moral development, and of those who do, many do not apply high moral development to every situation. In order to understand Kohlberg's stages, note that Kohlberg did not ascribe moral judgment to the final decision, but to *how* the person made the decision. Kohlbergs's stages of moral development are:

- Stage One: Obedience/punishment orientation—In this stage, behavior is controlled externally by rules and people in authority. This stage is ascribed to young or shallow thinkers, people who obey rules because they are told to do so and fear punishment for not following rules. The individual does not actually think about the rule, why it exists, or whether they agree or disagree with it. Children in Stage One may decide not to bully because they fear punishment from parents, teachers, or other adults. Alternatively, they may bully because they see others bullying and they do not think that there are any consequences for bullying. Rules against bullying are sufficient to prevent bullying by children in Stage One moral development.
- Stage Two: Naïve hedonistic or instrumental orientation—In this stage, behavior is driven by external rewards or gains. A child in Stage Two may bully because bullying makes him feel powerful or in control, provides snacks money, or other items from the victim, or provides attention. The child in Stage Two may decide not to bully because the school offers incentives for positive behavior. Age-appropriate rewards distributed fairly and justly to youth who do not engage in bullying may be sufficient to prevent bullying the child in Stage Two moral development.
- Stage Three: Good boy/Nice Girl morality—In this stage, behavior is controlled by others' perceptions of actions. The child in Stage Three considers how others will perceive bullying. Will bystanders be im-

pressed by the attacks, believing the bully has power and influence or will they have contempt for the bully? In Stage Three thinking, the bully attacks when he or she perceives that others will respect bullying. Deconstructing the myth that bullies are respected and holding open, honest discussions about how classmates feel about bullying and bullies may dissuade some Level Three thinkers from bullying. It is not enough to use negative stereotypes to combat bullying. Schools can maximize the Good boy/Nice girl mentality by encouraging and recognizing students who promote the social well-being of the school community. For example, recognizing the students who reach out and befriend students who are new or different reduces bullying in ways that go beyond disparaging bullies.

- Stage Four: Law and Order orientation—In this stage, behavior is controlled by official mandates. Stage Four morality is common in military and quasi military organizations, where low to high ranking personnel accept authority without question. Children in Stage Four of moral development may be deterred from bullying by those in authority. Informational presentations by the school disciplinarian, principal or local police officer may prevent bullying in this group. Law and Order presentations should be used with caution because they have very limited application. The natural process of adolescent rebellion may cause teenagers to reject presentations from authority figures which increase bullying. Furthermore, bullies have an underlying sense of entitlement. Bullies may ignore statements by those in authority because bullies believe that they are the authority. Instead of following directives, bullies assert themselves as leaders and use the law and order mentality to direct others.
- Stage Five: Social Contract orientation—In this stage, behavior is determined by social contract. People behave according to unspoken concepts of what is necessary for the good of the community. The social contract is dynamic and can adapt itself based on the perceived needs of the social group. If an organization actively supports bullying, as in the hazing of new recruits to military groups, bullies may believe that they have a duty to harass others, and that bullying is part of the social contract. A true social contract honors basic human rights to life and freedom. Contracts can be used in the classroom by having all members of the class develop, and agree on, rules against bullying. Social contracts can be very successful with adolescents. Developing a written social contract against bullying, agreed on and signed by all members of the class, team, or club, is an application of Stage Five morality.
- Stage Six: Universal ethical principle orientation—In this stage, behavior is determined by internal values of justice, beneficence, and

> respect for persons. Justice is equal rights and benefits for all people. Beneficence is to act with goodness toward others. Respect for persons is to treat others with dignity, kindness, and esteem. The moral principles are abstract, rather than concrete. The person who employs Stage Six thinking serves as a defender of victims, regardless of who the victim is, what the victim looks like, or where the victim comes from. Schools can promote universal principles. However, in order to be successful, universal ethics must be applied at every level. Schools that advocate respect for others and then use automatic suspension or expulsion are sending mixed messages. Ethical principles must be honored at every level; they cannot be selectively employed.

Kohlberg's stages of moral development show that moral judgments are not so much about the choices that people make, but about how choices are made. Factors that influence the decision to bully are age, intelligence, life experiences, internalization of core values, and gender socialization. Bullying interventions must address the appropriate level of moral development of the target population. A major criticism of Kohlberg's work is that the model is based on a masculine perspective that values justice. Feminist perspective emphasizes honesty, compassion, and empathy, a field known as relational ethics. The underlying principles of relational ethics are a basic belief that all individuals are interrelated. Some populations are vulnerable to maltreatment and require special considerations. In order to provide ethical decisions, decision makers must be particularly attuned to details and the main goal should be protecting vulnerable individuals. Relational ethics is an evolving philosophy with the potential to provide further insight into the interpersonal dynamics of bully, victim, and bystanders.

Incongruent Styles of Relating

Much of the research in bullying focuses on either the bully or the victim. Few studies investigate interpersonal exchanges beyond the abusive incidents. Information on offender–victim relationships have been investigated in domestic violence. Some violence is believed to be the result of incongruent styles of relating (Evans, 2010). The perpetrator uses one style of relating while the victim uses a different style of relating. The discrepancies produce confusion, miscommunication, and false assumptions, which produce a cycle of abuse. Chapter One discussed styles of relating as one component of social health. The two main styles of interest with respect to abusive relationships are competition and collaboration. Competition is a way to compete for scarce or limited benefits or resources. Youth compete for a variety of goals, such as athletic or artistic competitions, adult attention, prizes, peer respect, dating partners, college placement, scholarships, or job opportunities. When two people with different styles of relating work together on a project, the bully-prone personality will seek vulnerabilities in others. In learning about other people's vulnerabilities, the bully can conquer the competition and secure the end result more easily. The competitive, bully-prone personality views other people as potential conquests. Core values of the bully are domination, control, and superiority. Victories can be achieved directly or vicariously, through other people. Direct victories endow the winner with the spoils of war, such as material goods, services, or the emotional pleasure of having more power than another person. Vicarious victories provide satisfaction because the failure of others reduces potential competition and upgrades the competitor's status. The competitor will always be on guard for other competitors seeking to move up the hierarchy. The need for power and control may be rooted in basic insecurities. The competitor maintains a high self-esteem in public as a shield against other potential competitors. The competitor, alone, is very weak and employs an "us against them" attitude to garner social support.

The collaborative personality is victim-prone. The collaborator uses a participatory style of relating, where each person is viewed as an equal partner. Core values of the collaborator are respect for persons, social justice, and goodwill. The collaborator experiences pleasure in the success of others and grieving at the loss or failure of others. The collaborator has a strong underlying sense of self and works with others to achieve a common good. The collaborative style is seen in many landmark social advances, such as philanthropy, science, art, and civil rights movements. Problems occur when one person approaches a potential relationship expecting competition and the second person approaches the same relationship expecting collaboration; the incongruence produces a winner and loser. In the beginning stages of the interpersonal relationship, people are typically in a mode of information exchange. The collaborator will intentionally or unintentionally reveal personal weaknesses in order to determine if the collaboration is a good match. The collaborator is looking for partners who can compensate for the collaborator's own weaknesses. The competitor is guarded and will reveal very little about personal weaknesses. Instead, the competitor gathers as much information as possible about the collaborator, whom he views as a potential competitor. Information is power because it helps plan and develop the most effective and efficient mode of attack. To summarize, the collaborator is open and trusting, increasing vulnerability for attack and the competitor is distrustful, guarded, and reserved, reducing vulnerability for attack. If information exchange is not forthcoming or insufficient, the competitor may resort to deceit in order to facilitate information exchange. Common strategies are to feign sharing information, mock friendship, or gifts. These fake participatory actions serve several purposes, they hook the naïve collaborator into believing that the competitor is sincere in establishing a relationship and they promote the competitor's image among outsiders and bystanders, reducing bystander likeliness of getting involved once the bully starts abusing the victim. The victim is highly vulnerable to attack because the competitor enters the relationship with the intention of subjugating the victim.

Neither style of relating is superior to the other. People transition between the two styles, employing the appropriate style to the appropriate situation. During a sporting event, the competitive approach is desirable because competition increases cohesiveness among supporters and motivates the athletes. After the event, the collaborative approach can improve knowledge to weaknesses and promote future success. If athletes continued with solely competitive strategies, they may experience feelings of loss, failure, or distrust, which would impact mental health and future success. Problems occur when (1) one or both parties assume that the other party is approaching the relationship from the same paradigm or style of relating; (2) when one person suddenly and unexpectedly changes paradigm during the course of the relationship; or (3) when the situation requires a specific paradigm and the incorrect paradigm is applied. In some domestic violence situations, one person is stuck in the competitive style and the other person is stuck in a collaborative style. This is why domestic violence victims and, possibly, bullying victims, stay in abusive situations long after friends and family members tell them to get out. The victim lives in hope that the offender will change to a collaborative style of relating. In reality, the bully is unable to engage in a collaborative style. To the bully, the victim's style of relating is weak and vulnerable. Teaching children different styles of relating from an early age and how to apply different styles to different situations may minimize bullying as well as other types of abusive relationships.

Henchmen: Why Others Obey the Bully

During the German Holocaust, an estimated 10 million people of Polish, Greek, Dutch, Hungarian, Romanian, Italian, Russian, Jewish, and other ethnicities were killed. How much the German people knew of the mass genocides is unclear. The public was aware that certain people, religious minorities, homosexuals, and people with disabilities were being systematically persecuted. The Nazi party held legitimate power and few Germans questioned the racist actions and policies. Yale psychologist Dr. Stanley Milgram was perplexed by the degree of complacency among the German people. Milgram and his research assistants set out to study *conditions of obedience,* why people follow those in authority without question even when they know that the person in authority is acting in ways that are repugnant. The research group performed a series of experiments where participants were instructed to give another person a series of electric shocks. The authority figure instructed participants to increase the intensity of the shocks. No electric shocks were actually given. However, the participants did not know this. The person receiving the shock, a paid actor, responded to the shocks with screams of agony. Some participants were upset by the pain that they appeared to be inflicting and paused to ask if the experiment was completely necessary. Despite their concerns, many continued to administer the shocks as instructed. The researchers found that many participants delivered the maximum dose of 450 volts, three times in a row. Milgram's research and subsequent studies found that approximately 6 out of 10 people will follow the directions of an authority figure even though they feel that the actions are harmful or unethical. Milgram theorized that this unquestioned acceptance of authority may have developed through natural selection. People are dependent on other people for resources, food, shelter, and protection from harm. People who obey social leaders are less likely to get expelled from the group and are more likely to stay alive. In order to stay alive, it may be necessary for a person to transition from a state of free will to a state of social obedience. Milgram called the state of social obedience *agentic state* (Milgram, 1963). In bullying, follower and supporter henchmen are often in an agentic state. Followers do things that they might not necessarily do if they were operating under their own free will.

Genovese Syndrome

Kitty Genovese was a bar manager who was fatally attacked on her way home from work in the morning of March 13, 1964. Her attacker stabbed her in the back and ran away when a neighbor shouted out the window. Although multiple people heard her screams, none came out of their homes to help. Genovese staggered a short distance where she collapsed, out of sight. Her attacker returned, wearing a hat to hide his face. He stabbed Genovese until she could no longer fight back and, then, raped her. At least one dozen neighbors witnessed Genovese's assault and failed to help her or call for the police to help. An investigative reporter with the *New York Times* (Gansberg, 1964) was horrified by the apathy of her neighbors. He reported the lack of response as extreme callousness by New York City residents. The news article was later criticized for reporting biases. However, it served to highlight a disconcerting issue that continues today—the indifference of bystanders.

Genovese syndrome is a term used to describe the failure of bystanders to act in cases where there is a need. There are a variety of reasons why bystanders may not act: (a) fear of harm; (b) a desire to avoid interactions with police or other authorities; (c) concerns that getting involved will require time and effort; or (d) a lack of problem-solving ability, an inability to determine what to do. After the Genovese incident, John Darley of New York University and Bibb Latané of Columbia University studied what became known as the Bystander Effect. The researchers believed that the witnesses of Genovese's attack did not call the police because they saw other neighbors watching the attack. The neighbors assumed someone else would call or had already called for help. From this, the researchers theorized that the greater the number of bystanders present during an emergency, the less likely it would be that one person would intervene. The researchers developed a laboratory experiment to study bystander effect. Participants were instructed to discuss the pressures of college life with other participants through an intercom system (Darley & Latané, 1968). The researchers explained that the purpose of the intercom system was to provide anonymity to discussants. Instead, the researchers played the participants a tape of someone pretending to have a convulsion. The researchers found that participants who thought that they were the only bystander witnessing the seizure were two to three times more likely to contact the research assistant to help the victim than bystanders who thought other witnesses were present. There were no differences with respect to the gender of participants. The researchers also discovered that the bystanders who did not report the medical emergency did not show signs of apathy. Many of those who did not act later asked the research assistant if the participant who seemed sick was now OK. The belief that one does not have to act because others will act was named diffusion of responsibility.

With diffusion of responsibility, the liability for action or inaction is diffused across a larger group of people. Each person feels less pressure or duty to act. The concept of diffusion of responsibility is used in firing squads. Procedurally, one shooter is given a blank or dummy cartridge and the other shooters are given live ammunition. None of the shooters know who has the blanks and who has live ammunition. Each soldier believes that he shot the blank and responsibility is passed onto others in the group. In the same way that each member of the firing squad feels less culpable for the death of the victim, bystanders feel less liable for the well-being of victims of bullying. Alone, the majority of bystanders (85%) will help the victim. In a group of three or more, only about a third of bystanders will help the victim (Darley & Latané, 1968). The bystander effect has been demonstrated in action multiple times throughout history. In Nazi Germany (1933–1945), more than six million people were persecuted, tortured, and murdered. In Rwanda (1994), the overthrow of the Tutsi monarchy triggered the murder of more than half a million people and near extermination of the Tutsi people. The lack of plans and delays in evacuating low income families from New Orleans before Hurricane Katrina (2005) resulted in numerous waterborne illnesses. One way that victims can overcome the bystander effect is to single out specific bystanders. Calling out the name of a bystander and asking for assistance during an attack may prevent the bystander from shirking responsibility.

Subsequent studies of the bystander effect showed that bystanders decide how to respond based on how they see others respond. If one person responds with nonchalance, the others will show nonchalance. Bullies, who are very good at reading and initiating social cues, use this behavior to their benefit. The bully will act as someone in authority and direct bystanders to serve as henchmen, lookouts, or diversionary personnel. This process supports a pluralistic ignorance, where bystanders believe that social norms condone bullying when, in reality, the majority of the bystanders do not like bullying. Bystanders are silenced through a social process. Discussing feelings toward bullying as a society and teaching bystanders how to respond to bullying are ways in which adults can reduce the bystander effect.

Institutionalized Bullying

Bullying is so deeply ingrained into the everyday interactions of some organizations that it seems that they would not be able to function without bullying. In such organizations, legitimate power is abused. Many times, the bully is in middle- to low-management positions. The bully does not have good people management skills and uses the bullying as a way to maintain power. Bullying is common in organizations with a hierarchy, such as fraternities, military forces, police departments, health care, and academic institutions. Attacks are typically initiated by those who are in the middle tier of management. The bully and henchmen join forces to torture the victim so that bullying increases group adhesiveness. Senior day, a generations-old tradition where high school seniors harassed or humiliated underclassmen, is one example of institutionalized bullying. Bullying ensures a rigid hierarchy of the classes. The hierarchy is useful for people who are incompetent. In a rigid hierarchy, people who are incompetent are held in their current position while those who are competent are powerless to advance above them. Attacks often commence when a new person enters the organization.

The pledges, newbies, orientees, or plebes are subjected to a series of abuses. New people are particularly vulnerable because they have not had time to develop a protective social network and are still gaining self-confidence, less likely to resist or counter the attacks. The degradations ensure that the newcomer is placed at the lowest level of the organizational structure. Existing co-workers are also held in position by the abuses. They are kept busy trying to deflect the abuse and unable to show promotion potential. Organizations experiencing rapid changes through downsizing, reorganization, or unanticipated growth are at risk for institutionalized bullying. The problem can easily escalate to a chronically abusive and poor work environment. The bullies may not have adequate education, morals, or psychological stability to know when laws protecting employees against harassment have been crossed. Those in the highest levels of the organization overlook the bullying, possibly in the belief that feigned ignorance protects them from legal or moral responsibility. Good workers leave the organization while incompetent workers stay. The abuse produces a highly dysfunctional work environment.

Disinhibition theory describes a natural phenomenon where people do not hurt other people out of fear that the social group will reject them (Levy & Nail, 1993; Wheeler, 1966). Bullying contradicts disinhibition theory. If bullies and henchmen followed disinhibition theory, they would not hurt other people. Bullies and henchmen would be afraid of what others would think of them. Bullies must overcome the process of disinhibition. One way to overcome the process is by making bullying acceptable in the work or school environment. When bullying occurs over and over, and leaders make little to no effort to stop the behaviors, members of the organization begin to accept bullying as a normal part of institutional life. Since everyone appears to bully, bullying is no longer considered abnormal. De-individuation is a process when individuals engage in abusive behaviors, such as bullying, because they believe that they are less accountable (Diener, 1976; Festinger, Pepitone, & Newcomb, 1952). The attackers may believe that they are immune from reprisal because everyone else is also perpetrating the behavior. Middle and upper level managers can unknowingly reinforce bullying by attempting to hide, downplay, or justify the abuse. Managers may exhibit the same behaviors as those performed by school authorities during the early, uninformed days of bullying prevention. The managers may suggest that the victim is overly sensitive, question whether the actions actually occurred, or infer that the victim did something to deserve the abuse. Authorities may be able to hide the behavior for a period of time, but eventually a pattern of abuse will surface and the organization will suffer from lawsuits, decreased work productivity or financial collapse. Training new and upcoming managers in good management techniques, promoting a collaborative work environment, and having good systems in place to address workplace bullying can maintain a positive and productive work environment.

The Community

Sociocultural theories are a category of theories that describe factors in the community which promote violent behavior. Two sociocultural theories that apply to bullying are resource theory and culture of violence theory. Resource theory (Warner, Lee, & Lee, 1986) describes how people with access and control of the resources are in a position of dominance and control. Bullying is one way to maintain control of resources. At Jena High School in Lousiana, students with white skin had power. The shade tree in the schoolyard was proof of that power. On hot days, white students sat under the tree for relief; black students did not. On an August day in 2006, during a school assembly, Kenneth Purvis asked the assistant principal if black students were allowed to sit under the tree (Shapiro, 2007). The administrator responded that the youth could sit anywhere they wanted. The next day, Kenneth and his cousin stood under the tree. Soon afterward, three white students strung nooses from the tree, a symbol of racism and hatred. Racial tensions increased, with fights between students with white skin and African American students. In a misguided attempt to stop the violence, the local district attorney and police officers went to the school and held an auditorium presentation. During the presentation, District Attorney Reed Walters threatened students with the statement, "I can make your lives disappear with a stroke of my pen" (Goodwin, 2007). The black students felt that Walters was looking directly at them when he made the statement. The coercion did nothing to stop the violence. The fighting continued. Students who were white received lighter penalties than students who were black, until media attention and civil rights leaders spotlighted the injustices. Thousands of people went to Jena to demonstrate the injustices. Eventually, public outrage pressured local leaders, and the charges against black students were reduced. The case of Jena High School shows how bullying can be used to maintain social dominance. The white students, the district attorney, and the local police held power in the community and did not hesitate to demonstrate their power. When the balance of power swung to support the black community, the white community of Jena did not know what hit them.

Culture of Violence Theory (Coser, 1967) proposes that people who are poor will resort to violence more frequently because violence is learned and accepted as a way of life. Some social issues, such as unrealistic expectations, strongly defined gender roles, criminal justice inequalities, and depersonalization increase the risk of violence-related behaviors (Rosenberg & Fenley, 1991). An example of how bullying works at the community level was the National Socialist German Worker's Party (Beck, 1999). The Nazi Party started as an attempt to draw the German people together after the humiliating defeat of World War I. The entire country was depressed and suffering from economic instability. The party increased national pride and improved the morale of the German people. Unfortunately, the pride was not harnessed appropriately and the pride grew into ethnocentric arrogance. The German people degraded and depersonalized those who were different. Millions of people were murdered through state-sponsored genocide. Cultural and national pride can be positive as long as the feelings are controlled, realistic, sensitive, and respectful to other groups. Culture of violence theory suggests that communities that are rigid and unable to accept and respect people who are different are at risk for perpetrating systematic violence.

The advantage of sociocultural theories is the identification of attitudes and environmental factors in society that support violence. By changing attitudes, increasing resources, and eliminating gender and racial disparities, it may be possible to decrease some violence and bullying. Schools regularly engage in efforts to increase school pride. Mascots, pep rallies, sporting events, and other activities encourage pride and school cohesiveness. It is important to note that these events, if uncontrolled, may also selectively isolate students who look, act, or speak differently. Schools can alleviate some violence by practicing social justice, supporting those who are different, and providing an inclusive and accepting environment.

CHAPTER 7

Treatment and Prevention

Medical professionals view health issues from two perspectives: the medical model and the public health model. The medical model focuses on diagnosis and treatment of the individual. If a person has a sore throat and a cough, the person goes to the doctor who cultures the throat, diagnoses an infection, and prescribes medications, if warranted. If the person experiences a reoccurrence or worsening of the sore throat, the person will return to the doctor, who will then reevaluate and revise the treatment. Treatment is a response to a specific problem. Depending on the doctor's training and personal attitudes of treatment, the patient may or may not have a say in the treatment. If treatment is solely dictated by the doctors, the patient has no say in the treatment protocol. This can be a problem if the treatment causes undesirable side effects. In the case of an upper respiratory infection, the patient may experience a stomach upset while taking antibiotics and may stop taking the antibiotic before the full course is completed. If all pathogenic bacteria are killed, the bacteria may grow back, this time with an antibiotic resistance, which is harder to treat. Waiting until problems occur and then responding to the problem is imprudent, reactionary, and expensive. The second approach to disease is the public health perspective. Public health professionals identify groups of people at risk for disease, work with members of the community to plan acceptable interventions, and evaluate the interventions to determine success. The public health approach attempts to prevent disease before it occurs. Public health focuses on the community instead of on the individual. Just as in individualized medicine, public health employs best practices or science-based treatments. The disadvantage of public health is that it is contrary to the core values of American society. Americans value independence, individualism, and personal strength. Public health depends on people caring for other people in society, not putting themselves first.

The public health approach separates people into three categories: (1) the universal population, people unaffected or marginally affected by the problem; (2) the selected population, people who have one or more risk factors of the problem; and (3) the indicated population, people who currently engage in the unhealthy behavior. The needs and treatment of these three groups are very different. Treatment and prevention efforts are also classified according to the three levels. Primary, or universal, prevention stops the problem before it occurs. Secondary, or selected, prevention identifies high-risk populations and intervenes to fix the problem and promote more positive behaviors. Tertiary, or indicated, prevention controls the worsening of the condition and complications. Effective treatment of issues, such as bullying, require the successful balance of primary, secondary, and tertiary efforts. Goals of public health are to minimize the factors that promote violence and maximize protective factors. Examples of public health interventions for youth violence are limiting exposure to violence by educating parents; early diagnosis, treatment, and prevention of mental health disorders; promoting healthy parenting techniques; increasing family–school connectedness; and empowering communities through social justice.

Emergency Medical Care

Attending to the immediate physical and emotional needs of injured persons is the first consideration of any intervention. First aid should be administered by the first people who arrive on the scene, regardless of medical training. Bystanders should focus on the physical and emotional needs of the injured. People who are not medically trained can help by notifying medical personnel. It is important to provide both physical and emotional support. Holding the injured person's hand and consoling the person sends the message that the injured party is important and cared for. Standing at a distance and waiting for medical professionals to arrive may be perceived as callousness and will exacerbate the trauma. Inaction sends a message that the person is not important or worthy of attention, which can add to the stress. Treatment is dependent on the type and severity of the injuries. The main priorities of first aid treatment are preserving life, preventing further harm, and supporting optimal recovery. Preserving life means taking care of problems in the correct order of (1) airway, (2) breathing, and (3) circulation, known as the ABC's of first aid. Respiratory and cardiac problems are treated before bleeding or broken bones. Preventing further harm means either removing the injury victim from the harmful situation or removing dangerous conditions from around the victim. Recovery is optimized by securing qualified and competent medical or mental health treatment as soon as possible after the event. Sources of qualified medical care are nurses' offices, emergency rooms, health clinics, or health care provider's offices. As the physical health of the victim stabilizes, the next consideration is helping the victim to heal from the trauma of violence. Victims will need additional assurances of safety and security to help their transition back to normal activities.

Emotional Support of Victims

Victims may need time to understand, accept, and develop a plan to deal with the violence. Initially, victims may be confused, in denial, and not ready to acknowledge the problem. Victims need time to go through the normal process of grieving. Victims experience multiple losses. They need to grieve the loss of respect, loss of social connections, loss of safety and security, loss of trust, and loss of educational or work opportunities. The stages that people go through in accepting losses are denial, anger, bargaining, depression, and acceptance. These stages were defined by Eleanor Kübler-Ross, a psychiatrist working with dying patients (1969). In the denial stage, the victim struggles with the idea that he was a victim. The victim may make excuses for the bully or voice contradictory statements, where sometimes behaviors were hurtful and sometimes they were not. The victim's uncertainty, combined with the bully's self-confidence, make the victim's accounts appear scattered and unreliable. Asking bystanders for their observations will minimize some of the ambiguity. As the victim moves through denial, he or she may be able to provide a clearer report of the events. Friends and family members can help move victims through denial by asking stage appropriate questions, such as: What behaviors did the offender exhibit? Did the offender cross personal boundaries?

During the stage of anger, the victim may direct the anger outward with antagonistic outbursts, counter aggression, or hostile behaviors, or inward with self-mutilation or suicidal behaviors. Friends and family members should not take the outbursts personally. It is not unusual for child victims of violence to demonstrate acting out behaviors, especially in places and with people whom they feel safe. Questions to consider are: Does the offender have power over the victim? Does the offender abuse this power? It may be unsafe for the victim to act out against the perpetrator. Friends can support the victim by allowing the victim to vent and then diverting attention toward positive activities. During the bargaining stage, the victim will attempt to make deals with the bully, friends, family members, or others. The victim may attempt to placate the bully, giving away prized possessions. The victim may make deals with parents, trying to get out of school in order to avoid interactions with the bully. People move through the stages at their own pace and can get stuck in a particular stage, or move through a stage very quickly, giving the appearance that the stage was skipped. It may help to ask the victim if there are other victims. How do the other victims respond to their bullying? How do bystanders respond? What do the bystanders think about the bullying? Is there anyone in a position of power over the bully and how does this person respond?

After bargaining fails, the victim experiences depression. During depression, the victim appears to become resigned to the abuse. At this point, the victim realizes that the bullying is real, intentional, and painful. The victim may withdraw from social groups, school, and family, feeling unworthy of other people's company. The victim may disengage, no longer acting as part of the school community. Many people consider suicide at some point in their lives. Death of a loved one, problems with relationships, or difficulty at home, work, or school can be very disturbing and can influence the way a person views his or her life. While these difficulties may seem overwhelming, they are usually temporary and fade over time. The problem is that the person experiencing the crisis is under such emotional strain that it is difficult to notice potential solutions. Friends, family members, and bystanders must take the initiative to reach out and help the struggling person. The first step for bystanders is to recognize the most common warning signs of suicide—threatening to hurt oneself or to commit suicide; investigating different ways to commit suicide; stockpiling drugs or guns; a preoccupation with death, either through conversation or writing; hopelessness, anger, loss of control; feeling trapped, anxious, or agitated; insomnia or sleeping all the time; recklessness; drug or alcohol abuse; withdrawing from friends, family, and society; wanting to be alone; giving away prized possessions; or rapid changes in mood. A rapid improvement in mood is also a warning sign since this may mean that the person has made a plan for suicide and is in the process of acting on that plan. If any of these signs are noted, the best approach is an honest, direct question, asking if he or she is considering suicide. A nonjudgmental, open approach encourages the person to express his or her feelings. The ensuing discussion allows the listener to understand the extent of the problem and to show compassion. Friends must also be careful not to get drawn into a conspiracy of silence. It is not a betrayal of trust to seek help for a friend in need. Encouraging the individual to talk to others, including qualified counselors about feelings of depression, helplessness, or hurt is what friends do. Friends must also realize their own limitations in attempting to help the person. A friend cannot make the sadness go away or stop the pain. Listening, supporting, and validating the pain are what is needed. The contemplator of suicide needs to express concerns and to feel that he or she is being heard. Mental health professionals, suicide prevention agencies, and suicide hotlines can guide supportive family members and friends until the individual is ready to seek help on his or her own.

Acceptance is the final stage. This is where the victim recognizes the bullying for what it is and endures the attacks, knowing that he or she may be in this predicament alone and that bystanders are either powerless to stop the bully or do not care enough to stop the bully. During the acceptance stage, victims can devise a plan to stay safe. Examples of plans might be to stand up to the bully, to tell a joke to diffuse the violence, to avoid the bully by taking a different route through the hallways or to and from school, to walk with a friend, to stay near the teacher at recess or near the bus driver on the bus ride home, to distract oneself from name-calling by singing a song, to ask for help from an adult, or to ignore the bullying. Depending on how close the henchmen are to the action, the victim may befriend some of the henchmen so it is less likely that they will join in the bullying. (This tactic should be undertaken very carefully since the henchmen could turn at any second and the attacks could be more severe.) The victim should keep a journal of incidents to see if there are specific factors that set the bully off and to prove to authorities that the abuse was chronic and systematic. It is important that the victim not fight back because bullies are manipulative and can influence school officials to punish the victim for counter attacks. The stages of grief have been applied to many illnesses and losses. Understanding that bullying victimization is a loss—a loss of respect and dignity—can help provide better supports to victims. The major criticism against Kübler-Ross's stages of grief is that the stages were developed based on observations, not by a formal research study.

Preventing Further Attacks

Once someone has been a victim, he or she is at high risk for subsequent victimization. Offenders seem to have a sixth sense for detecting vulnerable targets. Surveys reveal that violent offenders consistently spot the same people as easy targets. Once a person has been the victim of bullying, the person is at high risk for further victimization, either by the same bully or other bullies. Victims can reduce their risk by empowering themselves and refusing to be a victim. Using basic personal safety strategies, collecting evidence, building supportive friends, developing resilience, finding safe, enjoyable activities that nurture spiritual health, moving to a new job or school or counseling, can promote future safety.

Basic personal safety tips will vary based on the developmental age of the child. General safety tips are to avoid areas that are poorly supervised, to walk in small groups of three to four, to maintain a low profile, to walk with confidence, and to stick up for others who are being bullied. Bullies will only attack in places where they feel like they are in control. Avoiding areas that are poorly supervised, such as back streets, parks, video arcades, or malls, can prevent some victimization. Youth are advised to walk to and from school with a group of friends, and not to walk alone. The same is true for riding the bus. It is advisable to ride the bus with friends or to sit near the front of the bus where the bus driver can observe what is going on. Perpetrators who are acting out of frustration–aggression will go after whatever target immediately comes to their attention. By maintaining a low profile, not calling attention to oneself, one can avoid bullies who act out of frustration. It is important for the victim to recognize normal social boundaries, such as personal space, borrowing personal possessions, and topics of conversation. If someone crosses these boundaries, making the youth feel uncomfortable, it is good to get away from the person and situation. If friends cross personal boundaries, it is important to let them know that they have crossed boundaries. Youth should not share secrets, information that they would not want parents, teachers, or peers to know about. Personal secrets can be used as ammunition for emotional abuse against the victim. If someone does try to bully, it is best that the potential victim maintain composure, not act frightened, flustered, or upset, and walk away from the bully. Victims can practice responding to attacks with confidence. Finally, a good way to avoid victimization is to stand up for others. When someone else is being bullied, sticking up for the victim demonstrates caring, compassion, and strength. Strategies that are not recommended are carrying weapons, stun guns, fighting back, or verbally abusing the bully.

The Internet is the Wild West of the modern era. There are few limits on content or behavior. Staying safe online requires similar techniques to staying safe in the community. Internet users should avoid areas where bullies are likely to lurk. Some online games are particularly attractive to bullies. Griefers are online gamers who will entrap, threaten, intimidate, and torture their victims. Normally confined to the computer screen, they enter the child's world as a cyber playmate and quickly set less-experienced players up for attack. Other names for griefers are SNERTS, "Snotty nosed egotistical rude teenagers," or "Sexually needy, emotionally repressed trolls." Griefers don't play to win; they play to humiliate. Online users should maintain their own privacy while simultaneously realizing that anything that is put out on the Internet is not private. Internet users should not share passwords, only communicate with people that they know in real life, avoid posting personal information or pictures, review tags, disable unwanted tracking devices, and maintain a sense of reality about the Internet. A false sense of security that what is put out on the Internet is private or anonymous is naïve. It is possible to trace messages and youth can face disciplinary actions at school if electronic postings interfere with the educational process. In some cases, such as sexting, where sexually explicit pictures of one youth are shared with a boyfriend or girlfriend, the sender may face criminal charges for transmitting child pornography. People should only write messages online that they are willing to say or share in person.

If bullying continues, despite intervention efforts, it is important to document the incidents. Noting who bullies; henchmen, and bystander actions; where, when, how, and the circumstances surrounding the incidents can fulfill several purposes. Documentation can illuminate times and situations that are higher risk. For example, if documentation reveals that the bully attacks on days after holidays, the bully may be dealing with issues at home that cause him or her to act out in school. The victim or the victim's parents can give this information to adults so that they can maintain closer supervision after holidays. Documentation can also help with legal proceedings. Victims have the right to be free of sexual harassment and the right to protection against retaliation for reporting bullying. If a victim reports bullying and the school administrators fail to act or they do act and the bully uses the same information to hurt the victim further, there are legal steps that parents and victims can take to ensure safety at school. Every child has the right to a safe learning environment. Documentation can help determine whether obligations for safety are being met.

In some communities, bullying is endemic. For generations, wealthy or powerful youth were allowed to openly bully youth who were poor or considered undesirable. It is hard to say why the adults did not stop the bullying. They may not have cared. They may have thought that bullying was harmless or they may have benefited from the bullying. They may have been operating on quid pro quo, a Latin phrase which literally translated means what for what, an exchange of goods or services for equal goods or services. Overlooking the transgressions of wealthy and powerful youth may have helped the parents of the youth overlook transgressions by school administrators. Over time and with urban sprawl, these small, strongly interconnected communities have grown. But, they are still operating on principles from the past. Wealthy and powerful youth are still allowed to bully other youth because no one has had the guts to stand up to them. Jena High School in Louisiana may have been such an example. Students with light skin were treated differently than students with dark skin. Social injustices could be traced back for generations. It took a lot of courage and community support for the African American students at Jena High School to stand up against the abuses. Not all victims are able to take on that level of injustice. In cases where bullying is endemic and school administrators are not dynamic in solving the problem, the victim should carefully consider whether it is better to move to another school. It may be better to walk away than to fight the problem. Eventually, the bullies will get what is coming to them.

Healing after the Trauma

Recovering from the emotional and physical trauma of chronic bullying requires time, patience, and self-care. Survivors are encouraged to seek medical treatment or counseling as needed and to adhere to the treatment plan; take medications as prescribed; monitor and respond to undesirable symptoms; ask for help as needed; and develop a lifestyle that balances and supports all of the components of health, physical, emotional, intellectual, social, and spiritual well-being. Survivors should recognize negative messages that may have been induced by the abuse, such as feeling hopeless and worthless, wanting to end life, feeling anxious or sad, or engaging in strange or risky behaviors. Emotional health is severely stressed by the toxic nature of abuse, and it is not unusual for survivors to experience negative thoughts. When self-deprecating thoughts come to mind, the survivor should deconstruct the messages. Are the messages true? Is this something that would be appropriate to say about another person? Is there any benefit to these messages? It is easier to break down negative thoughts before they become overwhelming. Negative messages should be replaced with positive messages. The survivor can do cognitive exercises, such as listing five strengths, five positive attributes, and greatest achievements (Copeland, 2002). Survivors should develop positive self-messages and repeat the messages over and over when they are feeling bad. Survivors should avoid making any major decisions during the recovery period. They may not be thinking clearly, and if they do need to make decisions, it is good to consult with a friend or loved one, someone who has their best interests at heart. Impulsive or poorly thought out actions may cause later regrets. Survivors should avoid people who make them feel bad about themselves. Surrounding themselves with supportive friends, friends who say nice comments, will support recovery. A healthy diet, exercise, good personal hygiene, fun and healthy activities, and learning new skills or information will promote a balanced lifestyle. One of the best ways by which survivors can heal is by helping others. Taking care of pets, children, elderly, or other disadvantaged members of the community helps the survivor to feel needed, wanted, and important and takes the focus off of past traumas.

Developing Supportive Friendships

Multiple studies indicate that the lack of supportive friends is a risk factor for victimization. Some bullies will even use feigned friendships as a way to gain inside information on the victim's vulnerable points. The bully lures the victim into a false sense of security, finding out about the victim's personal weaknesses, fears, or shames. Getting to know the victim identifies appropriate weak points and allows the aggressor to test different methods of attack, without alarming the victim. What is a putdown for one person is not necessarily a putdown for another. The bully needs to know what works and what does not work to hurt the victim. A second function of befriending the victim is that onlookers are less likely to get involved because they will perceive any problems as interpersonal dispute. Bystanders will assume that the dispute will be resolved and the pair will go back to being friends. Intervening in a dispute between two friends would be a waste of time and could potentially alienate the bystander when the friendship is re-established. The perceived friendship will also delay the victim from seeking outside assistance. The victim is confused, believing the aggressor was a friend. The victim may either feel responsible for the attack or is embarrassed to admit the vulnerability to another person. Helping children to recognize and develop meaningful, healthy relationships can protect against bullying.

The need to belong to a social group is instinctive. Social groups promote survival by protecting individual members from attack and by working together for food and shelter during times of hardship. In childhood, friendships allow children to practice social relationships, providing lessons for later life. Friendship is the state of being friends. Friends share affection, trust, and respect. Friends care for one another. Among all age groups, friendships are dynamic, which means friendships change over time. During adolescence, networks change very rapidly with one-third of the adolescent's friendships changing over a three week period (Cairns, Leung, & Cairns, 1995). Some friendships grow and flourish, while others diminish until they cease to exist. Researchers defined the characteristic steps of relationship building. The steps are (1) acquaintance; (2) buildup; (3) continuation; (4) deterioration; and (5) termination (Levinger, 1983). The acquaintance stage is at the initial meetings, where both parties exchange information in order to determine if compatibility and shared interest exist. People who do not feel a personal connection at this stage stay as casual acquaintances. Both parties know each other but do not share a great deal of personal information. During the second stage, buildup, the parties discern whether they want the friendship to advance. Both parties work to establish trust and respect. They share time, conversation, and activities. Buildup requires commitment to the relationship. Building up too rapidly without establishing trust can set a person up for bullying. Revealing fears, concerns, or personal secrets provides the bully with information on vulnerabilities, which can later be used to hurt the victim. The third stage, continuation, occurs as the friends share experiences, concerns, and accomplishments. True friends communicate well and show acceptance, empathy, and respect for one another. Each person works to understand the other person's perspective and gives the other person the benefit of the doubt in times of misunderstandings. Each person gives equally and fairly

Bullying can be prevented by building caring communities where individuals respect and value others. (Carlosphotos/Dreamstime.com)

to the relationship. Individuals in the continuation stage support each other through personal difficulties. Friends in the continuation stage stand up for one another, even during bullying. Friends do not turn their back on their friends. Deterioration occurs when one or both individuals become bored, disillusioned, or irritated with the relationship or the other person. The pair grows apart and communication diminishes. Depending on the circumstances and reasons for the deterioration, trust and respect may be maintained or lost. Friendships can rebound from the deterioration stage, if both parties are willing to work on the relationship. One person, alone, cannot fix a broken relationship. Repairing a broken relationship must be a mutual process. Trust and respect are at the heart of any relationship. Once trust and respect are lost, it is very difficult to mend the relationship. Termination stage occurs when the relationship ends. Some relationships end through death, moving, legal separation, or normal development, as people move onto other stages of life, such as going away to college.

While social integration is a valuable way to reduce victimization, the quality of relationships is more important than the quantity of relationships. People in relationships make a formal or informal pact to respect, encourage, and support each other. The rights of a relationship were developed to help partners struggling with relationships (Evans, 2010). The rights of a relationship are applicable to friendships as well as dating partners. In any relationship, each person has the right to:

1) his or her own point of view
2) have feelings and experiences recognized as real
3) voice concerns
4) have work, efforts, and interests spoken of with respect
5) encouragement
6) emotional support
7) clear and honest answers to questions or issues that concern him or her
8) a sincere apology for offensive words or actions
9) be asked respectfully, not commanded or ordered.

In relationships, each party has the right to individual identity, feelings, and experiences. Mutual respect of these rights is the sign of a healthy relationship.

Offender Services

Although the nation pays a lot of money to house offenders in the criminal justice system, there is very little funding for offender therapy in communities. Part of the reason for limited resources is that victim advocacy groups feel that the few funds that are available should support victims, not offenders. A second reason for the lack of services is that many offenders do not actively seek treatment. Some offenders, especially narcissists, don't think there is anything wrong with them. A final reason is public perceptions of offenders. Offenders are frequently seen as incorrigible, beyond hope. Offenders who are acting out of narcissism or suffering from antisocial personal disorders may not be treatable. Because there has been little funding and research into offender therapy, there is little information on what works or what might work to treat bullies. There is plenty of evidence showing that many of the current treatments are ineffective and may actually cause more harm than good (U.S. DHHS, 2001). Popular and ineffective strategies are boot camps, where delinquent youth are sent for pseudo military training, group therapy, residential treatment, and shock programs, such as scared straight. Boot camps do not work because they mainly focus on physical training, not on emotional skills. Group therapy is contraindicated because gathering delinquent youth together allows the youth to model and teach each other even more delinquent behaviors. When antisocial youth are gathered together and pro-social youth are excluded, the group redefines what is normal. They share ideas, suggestions, exploits, and tricks. The group becomes a training ground for even worse behavior. Shock or scared straight programs are also ineffective because the adults use bullying to stop violence. The adults in scared straight actually teach youth how to bully. Youth exposed to Scared Straight have higher rates of re-arrest. Many of the offender therapies for bullies are modeled on these ineffective programs.

Some offenders *do* recognize that they have anger management issues and want help. Offender treatment helps the bully or violent perpetrator to examine the underlying reasons for abusive behaviors. History of victimization, exposure to violence in the home or community, and undiagnosed learning disabilities are some common factors promoting violence. Discovering the reason behind the behaviors can help perpetrators to pause before acting and consider if these are behaviors that they really want to continue with. The major components of effective offender treatment programs are recognizing and giving up feelings of entitlement; developing appropriate ego strength; taking responsibility for actions; promoting openness to constructive feedback; feeling appropriate levels of shame or guilt; conscience formation; early recognition of physiological responses to anger; and self regulation of emotions.

Feelings of entitlement allow the bully to cross personal boundaries. Recognizing normal and healthy boundaries can help bullies to self-limit abusive behaviors. In interpersonal relationships, no one deserves (Evans, 2010):

1) inappropriate accusation or blame or constant and unwarranted criticism or judgment
2) words or names that humiliate, belittle, or devalue
3) emotional, financial, or physical harm or threats of harm
4) chronic anger or struggle for control
5) the silent treatment or threats of abandonment.

When someone does any of these, he or she has is no longer acting appropriately. Boundaries of trust and respect are being violated. It is the responsibility of the offender to stay within appropriate boundaries. It is not the responsibility of the victim to ensure that the offender acts responsibly.

Building Empathy

Empathy is the ability to understand why other people act or feel the way that they do. Bullies are able to overcome normal social inhibitions against hurting others because they perceive hostile intent where there is none. They automatically jump to offensive actions when they don't need to. Offenders can develop a rational and kinder approach toward others by building empathy. Helping the bully to see the circumstances from the other person's perspective increases the bully's empathy. Many violent perpetrators only see incidents from their own perspective. They believe that they are the victim, downtrodden by life's circumstances, or being ridiculed by the other person. Empathy building exercises use role playing exercises to help the bully see and feel the victim's experiences. Building empathy requires self-reflection of past behaviors. Self-reflection requires the perpetrator to understand what the victim is experiencing and the consequences of the abuse. Through these exercises, the bully will realize some of the many negative outcomes of his or her actions. The abuse creates emotional and physical distance between the perpetrator, victim, and bystanders. Victims and bystanders distrust the bully. Some bullies, particularly provocative victims, experience guilt, shame, and embarrassment. The bully may lose rights, such as recess, free time or the riding the bus, if authorities intervene. Encouraging the bully to name some of the negative outcomes of his or her behavior may promote a change in the behavior. Empathy development will not work for all bullies. Some bullies are resistant to empathy building because they see empathy as a weakness. Some programs attempt to include the victim in the empathy-building process. This may put the victim at greater risk because the victim may expose weaknesses that can be used as later ammunition by the recalcitrant bully.

Teaching bullies to recognize personal triggers, those events, incidents or circumstances when they feel upset or hurt can alert bullies to potential incidents. The bully who acts out of frustration–aggression can self-soothe to allay self-defeating violence. Anger is an emotion that occurs when a person feels wronged, threatened, or harmed without adequate justification. Anger, itself, is not a problem. Emotions, including anger, are a normal part of life. Anger becomes a problem when it is combined with hostility and aggression. Hostility is an antagonistic view of the world, other people, or situations. Hostile people assume that others are hurting them, intentionally, when they are not. The views of hostile people are distorted and not consistent with reality. The hostile person assumes malicious motivation when there is none. Aggressive responses are behaviors, such as verbal abuse, threats or attacks, that are meant to hurt others. Bullies who exhibit anger, aggression, and hostility may benefit from anger management programs.

There are different types of anger management programs. Currently, the most successful programs are cognitive behavioral therapy programs, delivered individually or in small groups. Cognitive behavioral interventions are interventions that help the person struggling with anger management to deconstruct hostile perceptions (cognitive) and to avoid aggressive reactions (behavior). The interventions are intended to change how participants see and interpret circumstances and to replace angry reactions with calm, thoughtful, and assertive responses. Because the goal of anger management programs is to change behaviors, programs are usually delivered over a period of several months. This time period allows the participants to practice and refine the techniques in daily life and to overcome relapses without giving up on the program. Anger management programs must be led by qualified mental health clinicians who are trained to understand the root causes of anger, able to set appropriate boundaries, and able to apply evidence-based practices. Poorly trained or inexperienced therapists can harm program participants and the participants' loved ones who often bear the brunt of the anger. All health professionals are bound by professional codes of practice that require them to report cases where a patient presents a threat to self or others. Experienced clinicians use techniques, such as setting ground rules for safety and confidentiality, to ensure the safety of the client and the client's current or potential victims. Effective anger management programs help clients to recognize anger and to channel the energy into positive, rather than negative, outcomes.

Cognitive behavioral therapies to help manage anger are relaxation techniques, cognitive interventions, and communication skills (Reilly & Shropshire, 2002). Relaxation techniques focus on helping the participant to recognize early signs of anger and to employ techniques to relax the body before the anger gets out of control. Each person has specific events or situations that trigger feelings of anger. Some common triggers are having a friend say bad things, having someone take something without permission, or getting into trouble for something that someone else did. Recognizing the circumstances that cause anger helps the participant recognize high-risk situations when they occur. The next step is to be alert for the physiological signs, such as a clenched jaw, increased blood pressure or heart rate, reddened face, or shallow breathing, and behavioral signs, such as pacing, clenching a fist, yelling, or punching a wall. In addition to recognizing the situations, physical signs, and behavioral signs of anger, it is helpful to identify the underlying emotions that often go along with anger, such as fear, hurt, or jealousy. The last piece of relaxation training is to practice and learn techniques that help the participant feel in control again. Common relaxation techniques used in anger management are taking timeouts, exercise, talking to a friend, progressive muscle relaxation, and deep breathing. Cognitive interventions help the individual to recognize irrational beliefs or typecasts that agitate anger. Cognitive therapy helps the participants to recognize destructive thoughts and to stop or reframe the thoughts before they react. Developing good communication skills helps the individual to differentiate between responses that respect the other person and responses that hurt or diminish the other person. Assertiveness training helps people to stand up for themselves without hurting others. Successful programs employ multiple strategies to help the person recognize high-risk times, control thoughts and actions, and to resolve conflicts in ways that respect all parties.

Bystanders

Bystanders are instrumental in determining the frequency, severity, and extent of bullying attacks. Bullies would not bully if they thought that bystanders disapproved of attacks. The reality is that most bystanders, approximately 8 out of 10, do disapprove of bullying. Most people do not like bullying. They do not like seeing other people being hurt. Yet, in public, bystanders appear to respect the bully. This is not a true respect. They are merely pretending to show respect because they do not want to become the next target. Bystanders prefer to distance themselves from bullies. Some bystanders have the courage to tell bullies that they don't like bullying, though many do not. For bystanders who are unwilling to stand up to the bully, there are other strategies. Bystanders can use physical distances and proximities to support victims. Rather than moving away from the victim during bullying incidents, bystanders can move closer, using body language to show victim support. Bystanders can frown, looking disapprovingly when the bully first advances toward the victim, stand, leaning in toward the victim, or stand between the victim and the bully, or henchmen. If the bystander does not feel comfortable getting involved at this level, they can tell an adult or supervisor. If the person supervising does nothing, they can go tell another adult and continue telling other adults, until one of them does something. Older bystanders can document what is going on and send anonymous messages to administrators. Noting who, where, what, when, and how incidents occurred, will help authorities to intervene effectively. Reports should be honest and factual. Exaggerations undermine the message and authorities may not take the report seriously. If bystanders note certain times and places where the victim is more vulnerable, they might try to draw the victim away from those situations. Simple strategies such as making sure that the victim is not alone will make bullying more difficult. Recruiting other bystanders into supporting the victim will share responsibility and provide better coverage against bullying. Bystanders who don't feel comfortable doing any of these can still support victims by contacting the victim outside of school, letting him or her know that what is happening is not right, and that not everyone in the school, class, or community feels the way that the bully does. Letting the victim know that what is happening is wrong can reduce some of the victim's self-destructive thinking. Assurances and concern for the victim can be a powerful mediating factor in preventing suicide or homicide. Bystanders who stand up for victims are heroes in the eyes of the victim.

The Role of Parents

Discussing Bullying and Expectations of Behavior

Discussions regarding how children are expected to treat others, what to do if they are the victim of bullying, and what to do if they observe another child being bullied provide a foundation for pro-social behavior. A good time to start the discussion is when a child is starting school or seeking new rights, such as the right to play with friends without adult supervision, the right to use the Internet, or the right to have a cell phone. This is a time when parents can help youth to understand that rights come with responsibilities. There are many great resources to help guide discussions between parents and children. Examples of general questions for parents to use with children are (Substance Abuse and Mental Health Services Administration, 2008):

- What does bullying mean to you?
- What do you do at recess? Who do you play with?
- How is your bus ride (or walk to school)? Who do you sit (or walk) with? What do you do on the way to and from school? How does your bus driver handle children who misbehave on the bus?
- Do you ever feel lonely at school? If so, what is that like?
- Have you ever been afraid to go to school? What were the circumstances?
- Have you ever been hit, pushed, or called mean names at school? Have you ever had anything stolen? Has anyone ever made you feel like you don't belong to their group?
- Have you ever seen others being hit, pushed, or called mean names at school?
- Have you ever hit, pushed, or called another child mean names at school?

If there are indications that the child has been victimized, follow-up questions are asked to find out who is doing the bullying, the types of bullying experienced, actions by adults and what the child would like the adults to do about the bullying. If the child reports witnessing bullying of others, follow-up questions are to ask what types of bullying were witnessed, how the observation made them feel, and how they might try to help a victim of bullying. If there are indications that the child is bullying other children, appropriate follow-up questions might be to ask how those actions may have made the victim feel. Parents may also discuss the school's current efforts to reduce bullying, how the child feels about the school's efforts and programs, and what the child recommends. Discussing situations that may arise before they happen can help the youth discern appropriate ways to handle bullying situations when they occur.

Once the discussions start, the lines of communication must be kept open. Checking in regularly allows youth to talk about issues as they occur. Teenagers respond well to contracts because contracts respect them as individuals. For example, parents might wish to contract that the child will treat others with respect. The contract should be clear and specific. If the responsibilities are violated, the consequence will be a loss of that right (i.e. cell phone use, Internet use, or going to the mall alone) until the child has had time to consider appropriate and inappropriate actions.

Support in Building Positive Friendships

A close group of supportive friends can serve as a protective shield against bullying. Bullies are less likely to target a child whose friends will potentially defend the child. Thus, providing opportunities to develop close, supportive friendships is one way that parents can protect against bullying. Children can form friendships in almost any social setting. The most common sources of childhood friendships are same-age relatives, children of family friends, neighborhood, places of worship, extracurricular activities, childcare, and school (Fletcher, Troutman, Gruber, Long, & Hunter, 2006). Among children and adults, friendships are dynamic. They either grow or deteriorate, depending on the quality and frequency of interactions, temperaments of the two participants, and the ability to adapt to changes over time. Childhood friendships that are related to parental relationships, that is, children of friends of the parents or relatives, tend to be longer lasting than school friendships. Part of the reason for this is that, when the parents are friends with the other set of parents, there will be more opportunities for interaction. Friendships developed at school are more transient because the friendship dyad is often separated each year when children progress to the next grade level. Even without the hurdle of classroom redistribution at each grade level, less than one in six of adolescent social networks remain intact over one year (Cairns, Leung, & Cairns, 1995). Parents can support friendships outside of school by providing many, varied social opportunities for interaction with other children.

Preventing Violence-Related Behaviors

Inconsistent parenting, where the parent vacillates between harsh punishment and inattention, fosters the development of aggressive behaviors in children. Youth become frustrated and act out when they cannot figure out the normal limits of behaviors. Basic, good parenting techniques can reduce the need for aggression. The American Academy of Pediatrics (AAP) recommends specific techniques. Providing clear and consistent expectations, encouraging attempts at the desired behaviors, praising successes, careful listening, encouraging independent problem solving, and setting limits as needed are ways in which parents can raise children to become independent and assertive. Foreseeing times when youth feel challenged or frustrated can alleviate some desire for aggression. Children have difficulty learning actions that require multiple steps. These tasks may seem overwhelming. Breaking complex jobs into single steps helps children master one step at a time. Parents can reinforce desired behaviors by encouraging, acknowledging, and rewarding positive behaviors as soon as possible, during or after the task. Practices, such as caught being good, provide immediate reinforcement of desired behaviors.

If children test behaviors and cross boundaries with undesirable behaviors, parents are advised to use discipline strategies, such as natural consequences, logical consequences, time-out, and withholding privileges. Natural consequences occur when parents allow children to find out what will happen naturally as a result of the behavior. For example, the youth who bullies through social ostracism will eventually lose friends because the friends will start to question the stability of the relationship and seek social networks elsewhere. Logical consequences are consequences that are a logical consequence of behaviors. If a youth bullies another youth through name-calling, a logical consequence is to separate the bully from the victim. The bully cannot sit, work, or play near the victim in class, lunch, or at recess. Withholding privileges involves taking away a benefit, such as recess or an opportunity to attend a school trip or school dance. The privilege should be related to the action and should not be something that the child needs, or something that would threaten the child's safety. For example, lunch is not a privilege because food is a necessity. Riding the bus may be considered a privilege. However, if losing the opportunity to ride the bus means that the child must walk to school on a dangerous road, the bus is not a privilege, but a necessity. Withholding privileges is not the same as punishment. Punishment is harsh treatment or penalty intended to inflict pain or hurt. The idea is not to inflict pain, but to teach the child that there are natural and logical consequences to actions. Parents are advised to use discipline, not punishment. Discipline means to instruct, train, or study in order to shape skills and intellect. Discipline is controlled and orderly, based on developing a high moral character. Discipline promotes the ethical principles of tolerance, kindness, and charity, whereas punishment harms children and teaches them that it is acceptable to harm others. Time-out is the last strategy recommended for parents. Time-outs are typically used for young children, aged 2–5 years. However, many people need a time-out when they feel lost, frustrated, angry, or upset. Time-out allows people of all ages to take a breath, relax, and approach the situation in a better state of mind.

Restricted Access to Firearms

In reviewing school attacks, the U.S. Secret Service report noted that two common characteristics of school attackers were a history of bullying victimization and access to a gun (Vossekuil, Fein, Reddy, Borum, & Modzeleski, 2002). Guns influence how people act. Berkowitz and LePage (1967) found that when they placed a gun in a room where people were completing a survey, respondents answered more aggressively than if the researchers placed a tennis racquet in the room. The researchers called this tendency to act more aggressively the weapons effect. The combination of bullying victimization and access to a gun can be a lethal combination. To the person who feels disenfranchised and disrespected, guns provide a seemingly quick solution. Some people believe that guns provide power and respect. For victims of bullying, guns may be perceived as a way to quickly restore the balance of power. The adolescent brain is not fully formed. Teenagers rarely understand the long-term implications of using a gun to solve problems. Those who do use guns to take control may spend the rest of life in prison where they will have even less control.

Gun violence is difficult to prevent in American society because of the powerful political views regarding the individual right to bear arms. Thus, schools and medical professionals must find a way to balance opinions supporting guns in children's homes with youth safety. Gun violence is an epidemic in the United States. The number of gun deaths is astounding. In 2004, five people died in New Zealand due to firearms, 37 died in Sweden, 56 died in Australia, 73 people died in England and Wales, 184 in Canada, and 11,344 in the United States. A gun in the home is more likely to be used against someone from the household than against a home invader. Many pediatricians screen to determine children's risk for unintentional gunshot wounds by including a question on access to a gun on the annual physical exam. This universal screening technique identifies children who may be at high risk and prompts parents who own a gun to think about how and where the gun is stored. Schools may want to consider including such an item on as part of the state mandated physical exams for students. Schools should also consider what messages are sent to children through police-sponsored programs, such as Drug Abuse Resistance Education (D.A.R.E.). These programs may inadvertently model carrying guns in school. When students see other students respect a police officer who has a gun, they may feel that a gun will also provide them with respect. No one should carry a gun in school. The mere presence of a gun will cause youth to act violently (Berkowitz & LePage, 1967).

Limiting Exposure to Media Violence

Exposure to violence in the home, community, or media fosters violence-related behaviors. Exposure to domestic violence is believed to cause physiological changes in the developing brain, which increases the risk of dangerous behaviors, such as drinking alcohol, using drugs, having multiple sexual partners, and weapon carrying (see Chapter 6). Children growing up in violent homes continue the behavior in their own homes, as adults. Violence-related behaviors are transmitted from generation to generation. Exposure to media violence, violent video games, movies, and information on computers brings violence into homes that might be construed as relatively safe. Media violence has both short- and long-terms effects on the viewer. Short-term effects are priming, arousal, and mimicry (Huesmann, 2007). Long-term effects are observational learning, desensitization, and enactive learning. Priming is a process that prepares the viewer for violence. Images of objects which should be neutral trigger inherent or learned thoughts and actions. For example, the image of a gun triggers feelings of aggression. Arousal is a second process which occurs after priming. During arousal, the person misinterprets actions as hostile when they are not. If the person gets bumped or jostled on a bus, they might perceive the action as intentional and malicious when it was unintentional. Mimicry is a short-term process where children observe social behaviors and act those out. While the actual neurological processes are not fully understood, it appears that certain neurons are stimulated during the mimicry process. In inner city day care settings, it is not unusual for children as young as three to five years to mimic violent and traumatic behaviors, such as drug busts, intimate partner violence, or gun play. Observational learning, a long-term effect of media violence, is where the person merges characters, scripts, and behaviors into everyday life. The person practices the behaviors until they become part of his or her own persona. Desensitization is when the person is no longer emotionally moved by violent images. It is natural for people to wince when they see violence perpetrated against another person or animal. Empathy for the victim is a human reaction, even if the victim is an actor and the violence is scripted in a movie or television show. Over time, and with repeated exposure, empathy decreases. The viewer becomes desensitized to violence and no longer experiences disgust or abhorrence to violence. Enactive learning is the process where learned behaviors are reinforced. In video games, violence-related behavior is reinforced through point systems and perceptions of admiration from peers. Because of the multiple effects of exposure to violence, it is wise to restrict children's exposure to any form of violence. Since this may be unrealistic in today's society, alternatives are to carefully deconstruct images of violence and the effects of violence as soon as possible after viewing. Discuss images of violence with children and help the viewer to see that the images are not real and that real violence causes death, pain, and suffering. Alternatively, limiting screen time to less than two hours will minimize children's exposure to violence.

Educators

Attending public school has been likened to changing jobs every year. With each new school year, children are required to learn and adapt to a new work environment and a new, temporary boss. They must learn new behaviors and skills, likes and dislikes of the teacher, and interact with people whom they might not ordinarily hang out with for many hours a day. In order to adapt quickly and effectively to this new environment, youth test behaviors to see what is acceptable and normal. Administrators can minimize the stresses of grade change by preserving the connections of beneficial friendships. This means keeping helpful and positive friendship groups intact from grade level to grade level whenever possible. These friendships can prevent against bullying victimization.

Classroom Management

Teachers and teaching assistants can help smooth the process of classroom changes with grade level by establishing, and communicating, expectations. In the early days of the school year, the teacher should verbally poll the class for suggested rules and then facilitate a discussion of the rules. Members of the group, and particularly older youth, must feel that they are part of the governing body of the class. This ground-up approach increases the potential for acceptance and adherence to the rules. Rules should be phrased positively. For example, to prevent bullying, the rule might be phrased "Treat others with respect," rather than "No bullying." Bullying prevention experts suggest hanging lists of rules on the wall or practicing classroom procedures (Olweus & Limber, 2000). Posting rules on the wall provides a reminder of the agreed-on expectations and serves as a neutral reference. When a member of the class violates the rule, an adult or classmate may point to the poster and remind the offender of the rule. This takes some pressure off the person performing the correction. It may also be necessary to practice the rules so that the students know the practical applications. Having the students walk from the classroom to the lunchroom in an orderly, safe, and civil fashion, without pushing, hitting, or shoving is one example of practical application of rules. Adults must implement rules fairly and consistently. This means that every child is held to the same standards. Adults cannot look the other way because they are busy or because the violator is a favorite student or because they personally dislike the victim. The selective or inconsistent application of rules and sanctions confuses children. Rather than discerning that some people have greater liberty and justice, onlookers may assume that rules are flexible and will attempt to violate the rules themselves.

Adherence to classroom rules presents a different issue where many preschool and early elementary age children will report classmates for the smallest, often exaggerated, infractions. Some adults find this trait objectionable as it is difficult to follow up on every perceived infraction. When a child repeatedly reports a classmate for rule violations, the adults start to ignore the reports. As the case of Montana Lance demonstrated, it is important for adults to listen to children. One way to handle the tattle tale child is to ask the child to take a minute to discern whether the report is meant to hurt or to help. Teachers ask the child to consider whether they are telling to help or telling to hurt. Empowering the child to differentiate tattling from reporting ensures that valid concerns are expressed and addressed.

Adults need to balance expectations with flexibility and understanding. Under stressful situations or out of frustration, children will backslide or make mistakes. They will break the rules. Careful supervision helps to identify bullying before it gets out of control. Transition times, such as before or after the weekend or holidays, going to lunch or coming back from recess, are high-risk times. Whenever children have been out of the carefully monitored, environment of the classroom, they may act out or regress to undesirable behaviors. Teachable moments are those times when issues, questions, or topics arise that alert an educator to the need for correction. An incident as simple as one student making fun of a classmate who gets an answer wrong, is an opportunity to remind all students of the need for respect and collegiality. Ignoring a mean name, a cutting remark, or a nasty look can send the message that the teacher is oblivious and/or put-downs are acceptable. Correcting the behavior, quickly and respectfully in front of the onlookers, shows professional competence and models how to help someone who is being hurt. Some teachers eat lunch with their students or play with the children at recess because it allows the teacher to see what is going on outside of the classroom. Spending time with students in a relaxed, casual atmosphere also helps build camaraderie of the group, which may help with leadership. Promoting a cooperative learning environment, modeling respectful behaviors, and close monitoring of student behavior will do more to prevent bullying than the most expensive and popular program.

Handling Incidents of Bullying with Dignity and Respect

School staff are not likely to look for what they don't want to see. If the school district superintendent's child is bullying other children, adults are not likely to notice it or to get involved. The first step to getting adults on board is to define school safety as a common goal. All adults who work with children should be trained in recognizing the signs of bullying, the definition of bullying, how to intervene effectively, procedures for reporting, and local resources for mental health treatment. Proper training helps adults differentiate bullying from other, normal childhood behaviors. For example, it is normal for preschool and early elementary school children to run and hit on the playground. Young children frequently engage in active play. It is also normal for young children to fall and get injured during this type of play. A game of tag that results in an injury is not bullying. As children develop, they learn coordinated, organized activities. The hit and run behaviors are seen less until they emerge again during adolescence. It is not unusual for teenagers to try to get the attention of potential dating partners by hitting, pushing, or name-calling. The behaviors stop as the youth learns more appropriate ways to communicate with potential partners. A solid understanding of normal childhood development provides a good foundation for bullying intervention.

On the playground and in lunchrooms, where most bullying occurs, it is sometimes possible to identify bullying through body language. The bully or victim may posture as an offensive or defensive reaction. Posturing is when someone stands as tall as possible, holding their shoulders in a broad position in order to look larger than they actually are. Posturing is often used by combatants to physically intimidate the opposition. Bullies may use posturing to intimidate the victim into submission. It is sometimes possible to observe the fight/flight/freeze reaction by victims during bullying. The fight or flight reaction is a normal physiological reaction to stressors, such as bullying. The body resorts to survival mode by concentrating as much energy as possible on getting oxygen and nutrients to the skeletal muscles, the muscles needed to run and fight. This means shutting down oxygen to areas that the body deems as unnecessary, such as the gastrointestinal tract. People experiencing the fight or flight reaction will have an increased heart rate and respiratory rate. They will breathe fast and, possibly, shallow. They may become either flushed or pale, as blood vessels dilate and constrict to send oxygen to where the body needs it. The person will have dilated pupils and tunnel vision, which means they only focus on the object of interest. Auditory exclusion then occurs, which means the person may not hear the words of people trying to intervene. Muscles may tremor and appear tense. Hair on the neck may stand on end. The person appears ready to fight or run away.

When confronting the bully, the first step is to name the behavior as bullying. Giving the behavior a name makes it real and helps the perpetrator who is suffering from distorted thinking to see the behavior as others see it. Bully and victim should never be interviewed together. The bully has a strong personality and will walk all over the victim, manipulating the adults into blaming the victim. It is necessary to set ground rules during discussions with bullies. Common ground rules in working with bullies are no sarcasm, no attacks, no innuendo, and no assumption of the other person's motives. Sometimes adults default to bullying as a way to stop bullying. This strategy is completely contrary to how children learn. Bullying a bully only teaches the perpetrator and bystanders to work toward becoming a bigger bully. Adults must use respect when interacting with all children and adolescents. Feelings of entitlement and depersonalization of the victim will need to be deconstructed for the bully. Role-play can be used to help the perpetrator to build empathy. Open discussions in the classroom will help the bully to see that any perceived admiration from bystanders is false. Classmates do not like to see bullying. Encouraging the bully to reflect on his or her actions and to see that others do not like and support the actions are respectful ways to address the problem.

In working with victims, adults should listen carefully, avoid jumping to conclusions, or rushing for a fix. The victim must feel as if he or she is being heard. Since some children, particularly males, struggle with verbal communication, body language may reveal more than words. Observing posture, gestures, and facial expressions may yield additional insights. The bully will appear confident and strong. He or she may even smirk or laugh at the victim. Victims appear unsure of themselves. The victim has been severely abused by the bully's power. Asking privately what he or she would like as a consequence helps the victim to feel empowered. If the victim desires an apology, the apology can be facilitated, provided that the apology is honest and victim safety is ensured. It is important to be honest and open with the victim, otherwise the victim will lose trust in possible defenders. Once information has been gathered from the bully and the victim, henchmen and bystanders should also be interviewed individually.

Each school has a disciplinary policy. How discipline is meted out varies, depending on the offender, circumstances, and how the person in authority feels about the bully, the victim, and family members of each party. When one group of students is allowed to bully and another group of students is harshly punished for the same behaviors or retaliatory behaviors, injustices do not go unnoticed. The disparities in school discipline have long-lasting and deeply rooted implications. Students, parents, and entire communities lose trust in school staff. Since learning requires trust, trust that the teacher is telling the truth, trust that the teacher is grading papers fairly, and trust that children are safe while in the care of the school, distrust severely undermines the educational process. Without trust, students cannot learn. Furthermore, communities will retaliate against system injustices. Bystanders withhold information as a form of street justice. If the star athletes get away with bullying kids, why shouldn't the kid down the street? The lack of cooperation among bystanders makes it hard to intervene to stop bullying. Inconsistent discipline sends the message that it is acceptable to bully some children, which encourages bystanders to join in the bullying, making life for the victim unbearable. The best approach is to assume that many children will attempt bullying at one time or another and to treat incidents as educational opportunities. The focus should be on changing the behavior, not hurting the bully. Disciplinary codes must be applied fairly and consistently. No child, regardless of athletic ability, parent connections, community connections, or political connections, should be allowed to bully another child without consequences.

Bullying prevention is addressed by using the same techniques as good parenting, setting clear and consistent expectations, and modeling respectful, caring, and inclusive behavior. There is no magic program, no one conversation or guest speaker that will eliminate bullying. After incidents of bullying, adults must continue to monitor the perpetrator, victim, and henchmen. One meeting, conference, or discussion is not enough. Some adults express concern that eliminating aggressive behaviors among children who live in dangerous communities may put these children at risk. These children may be taught to *code switch*. Code switching is when a person acts differently, depending on what the circumstances warrant. Most people code switch. People act differently in church, around grandparents, or at a formal occasion than they do around close friends, on the streets, or playground. Code switching comes naturally. Teaching children that behavior in school may be different from behavior on the street can help them to function better in many social situations.

Threat Assessment

After an event, such as a school attack or suicide, adults, who previously underreacted to bullying, often overreact. Every incident of name-calling, fighting, interpersonal dispute, or threat made in anger is treated as a criminal offense. Retaliatory threats are treated as terrorism and children are thrown in jail for impulsive, thoughtless actions. While bullying behaviors are certainly not desirable, there is a fine line between appropriate and inappropriate reactions. Proper training helps alleviate the underreaction/overreaction syndrome. Early identification and treatment of depression can reduce school threats. In reviewing school attacks, the U.S. Secret Service recommended assessing any threat for level of risk. This threat assessment approach differentiates poorly constructed threats, where a hurt child blurts out an angry comment, from real threats, where there is a planned attack with the resources to fulfill the threat. The threat assessment approach provides guidelines for the various threat levels. Threat assessment is based on the knowledge that some people who make threats will never attack, some people who attack never make threats and some people will make threats and attack. Threat assessment differentiates the three groups so that each case is handled appropriately. Threat assessment looks at the vulnerability of the target to attack, lifestyle of the person making the threat, and ability to make to follow through on an attack. When a threat or attack occurs, psychological first aid addresses the immediate mental health and physical needs of perpetrators, bystanders, and survivors of traumatic events. Psychological first aid reestablishes a human connection, provides practical help, and connects survivors to social support systems.

Evidence-Based Programs

Evidence-based programs are programs that have been proven effective in research. Groups of researchers, experts, and practitioners review programs to determine which programs are effective for specific problems. In 2001, the U.S. Department of Health and Human Services, Centers for Disease Control, National Center for Injury Prevention and Control, Substance Abuse and Mental Health Services Administration, Center for Mental Health Services, and National Institutes of Health, National Institute of Mental Health produced *Youth Violence: Report of the Surgeon General.* The report provided background on youth violence, introduced the public health model as an effective overall strategy, and defined model and promising programs. The report identified three key areas for youth violence prevention, climate (bullying prevention), firearm prevention, and drug and alcohol prevention. Efforts to identify the best practices continued with the Center for the Study and Prevention of Violence (CSPV) at the University of Colorado at Boulder. CSPV reviewed more than 600 programs. The researchers found that of the 600 programs, only about 31 actually worked. Surprisingly, some of the most popular and commonly used programs were deemed ineffective or could possibly do more harm than good. For example, the researchers found that group therapy for young offenders could actually increase the risk of offending because the groups became an informal training ground for even greater antisocial behavior. Today, the National Registry of Evidence-Based Programs and Practices analyzes programs for effectiveness and lists the effective programs in a searchable database. Implementing evidence-based practices within an overall framework of positive classroom management ensures that the needs of all students are addressed. Researchers estimate that it would cost approximately $625 million a year to implement an evidence-based program, such as the Olweus Bullying Prevention Program in 125,000 public and private schools in the United States (Pereznieto, Harper, Clench, & Coarasa, 2010). Since the cost of school violence is $14.4 billion to $40.3 billion (Pereznieto, Harper, Clench, & Coarasa, 2010), this represents a savings of up to $39.7 billion per year.

The Olweus BPP is one of the few evidence-based programs to address bullying in schools (Olweus & Limber, 2000). The program is one of the most widely used bullying prevention programs. The goal of the program is to promote empathy among students and staff and to stop preexisting practices that unintentionally promote bullying. The main components of the program are formation of a committee to plan and implement strategies, a student survey to prioritize interventions, training for staff, monitoring high-risk areas, rules against bullying, clear and consistent consequences for bullying, weekly class team meetings within the classroom, and parent involvement. In research, the program has been shown to reduce bullying up to 20 percent when implemented with fidelity, which means the people who offer the program, implement it as the program author intended. The major criticism of the model is that it provides general, not specific, guidelines. The school staff are responsible for adapting the model to the school environment and the developmental level of the students. The program requires creativity and energy. It is not a simple one-size-fits-all model.

Pediatric Health Care Providers

Doctors and nurses in emergency rooms, schools, and pediatric offices are the frontline in dealing with violence-related injuries against children. A survey by the American Academy of Pediatrics (AAP) found that more than 50 percent of pediatricians recently treated a patient with violence-related injuries (AAP, 2008). Nearly all of the pediatricians surveyed felt that screening pediatric patients for risk of violence was important. Yet, only 33 percent felt comfortable screening for community violence. The benefit of screening is that the doctor or nurse can identify high-risk youth, educate children and parents on the hazards of violence, refer the child and family to mental health resources, if needed, and prevent injuries before they occur. In order to increase screening, the AAP developed resource materials for pediatricians and composed a policy that outlines the roles of pediatricians in preventing youth violence.

The *Connected Kids: Safe, Strong, Secure™* materials focus on building resilience throughout the child's development. The clinical guidelines start within the first month after birth, when pediatricians are encouraged to talk to parents about ways to cope with parental frustration, available support systems, and maintaining the parent's mental health. During toddlerhood, when the child is crawling and exploring, pediatricians are encouraged to talk to parents about maintaining a safe home environment, including reducing access to firearms. Discussions about bullying are suggested at the age of 6. Alcohol and drug prevention, issues highly related to violence-related behavior, are suggested at the age of 8. The clinical guidelines list questions for pediatricians to ask, such as "Have you been in any pushing or shoving fights?" If the child acknowledges physical fights, the guidelines provide recommended responses, such as, "There are other ways to avoid fights. Let's discuss some of these strategies" (AAP, 2006, p. 46). Between the ages of birth and 21 years, pediatricians are encouraged to discuss peer relationships, healthy dating, conflict resolution, suicide prevention, depression prevention, gaining independence, and transitioning to a new environment post-high school. Pediatricians are encouraged to use their skills and influence in the community to advocate for behavioral health services, protect children from firearms, support bullying prevention in schools, responsible television, cable and Internet programming, and evidence-based programs in schools and communities (AAP, 2009).

Laws

Laws against bullying are necessary to ensure a safe and productive learning environment. Anti-bullying laws typically address bullying during school events, on school property, or when using school property, such as the computer system or the computer network. Each law should contain a statement prohibiting bullying, providing a definition of bullying, a description of the type of behavior expected of students and staff, consequences for inappropriate behavior, a procedure for reporting as well as protection for those who report inappropriate behavior, a procedure for investigation and strategies for protecting the victim, referral to counseling for victims and perpetrators of bullying, procedures for follow-up reporting with the victim and their parent/ guardian, a method of tracking and reporting incidents for institutional purposes, a procedure for notifying the school community of the policy and publication in the student handbook. The benefit of laws against bullying is that they provide clear and consistent guidelines for implementation. Bullying is an offense that depends on an imbalance of power. Having clear procedures to recognize and respond to bullying improves reporting because bystanders and victims are not afraid of the unknown, how school officials will respond. Set policies also make it harder for bullies to divert blame onto the victim or minimize the offense. School laws are important in determining funding priorities. Since states have limited resources and bullying prevention programs are in high demand, the department of education administrators can prioritize which schools will receive supplementary funding by analyzing how serious schools are in addressing problems. For example, schools with clear policies and procedures and mechanisms for tracking indicate a clear knowledge and concern for the problem. States can also mandate funding for evidence-based programs, only.

Currently, 47 states have laws against bullying. The quality of the laws varies. Bully Police USA defined 12 criteria necessary for effective anti-bullying laws:

1) The law must specifically use the term "bully." Laws against harassment or hate crimes are not sufficient to protect against bullying.

2) The law must speak to the safety of individual students, not to the entire school environment. Building safety is not the same as bullying prevention.
3) There must be clear and consistent definitions for harassment and bullying.
4) Theoretical application is not enough. The law should include statements on how to apply the components.
5) The law should demonstrate a collaborative approach to bullying using evidence-based practices in bullying intervention and prevention.
6) The law should mandate, not suggest, evidence-based programs in bullying prevention.
7) The law should include a start date for policies and programs.
8) There should be protection for people who report as well as protection against false reporting.
9) The law should address parent and teacher liability for failure to act or protection for those who do act according to the policies and procedures for bullying intervention and prevention.
10) Laws should put an emphasis on counseling services for victims.
11) The law should specify mandatory reporting of incidents to school officials.
12) The law should include cyber-bullying.

States are graded according to these criteria. Grades range from A++, scored by New Jersey, Virginia, Kentucky, Delaware, North Dakota, Florida, Massachusetts, Georgia, Maryland, New Hampshire, and Wyoming, to F, scored by Michigan, South Dakota, and Montana. A state automatically scores an F if there are no laws against bullying.

Recommendations from the World Health Organization

The WHO looks at youth violence from a global perspective. The WHO recommends a holistic approach that focuses on eliminating the basic social problems that allow bullying to occur. Bullying is rooted in social injustice. The bully is allowed to torment victims. Bystanders do not intervene because the bully has greater power than the victim and is perceived as more important, socially. Social injustice occurs when one person or group of people has a greater burden of responsibility or has fewer resources than others in society. In the United States, social injustices exist in criminal justice, health care, education, and job opportunities. A prime example of social injustice is the lack of job opportunities for adolescents in impoverished communities. Youth from poor minority communities do not have the same educational and job opportunities as youth from wealthier communities. This social injustice causes some youth to resort to drug dealing as a way to earn money. Drug dealing is a very risky business. Dealers are at risk of robbery, shakedowns by authorities, turf wars, assault, intentional and unintentional gunshot wounds, and incarceration. Drug dealing brings guns into neighborhoods, increasing the risk for everyone in the neighborhood. Dealing becomes endemic as young children look up to dealers as role models of successful businessmen. Legitimately successful members of the community move out because effective systems are not in place to provide a safe, comfortable community. Job training, education, access to effective drug treatment programs, strong community infrastructure, and reduced exposure to violence can minimize many of the issues facing poor communities. To reduce social injustices, the WHO recommends preschool enrichment programs, social development programs, vocational training, increased high school completion rates, home health care visitation programs, parenting programs, youth mentoring programs, increasing home-school connectedness through home-school partnerships, improving neighborhood quality of life, reducing access to drugs and alcohol, increasing extracurricular activities, creating safe routes to and from school, eliminating poverty, reducing access to firearms, reducing exposure to media violence, and educational reforms (WHO, 2002). Supporting the physical, emotional, and spiritual health throughout the lifespan saves money, demonstrates social justice and responsibility, and minimizes youth violence.

Truth and Reconciliation

After the Amish schoolhouse attack, the Amish community came together to support the victims, the victims' families, and the perpetrator's family. The American public was astonished by this reaction. How could a community that had been hurt support the perpetrator's family? The Amish reaction to the massacre of children stood in sharp contrast to the fear, anger, and outcry for vengeance, usually seen after school shootings in the United States. The reason why the Amish reacted differently from others was that the Amish community is a small, tight-knit community with strong spiritual values. The spiritual practices and religious values of the Amish community helped them to see that the perpetrator was a tortured soul. The Amish also forgave because they believe that, in order to enter heaven, they must forgive others. In order for the community to heal, they needed to acknowledge the pain and to forgive the perpetrator.

The concepts of truth and reconciliation originated through South African efforts to safely transition from an apartheid state to a free and equal state. Between 1948 and 1994, South Africa was controlled by a white minority, known as Afrikaners. Over time, the Afrikaner government passed legislature and employed policies to deliberately stymie the rights of Black South Africans. The Afrikaners segregated residential areas, removing Black South Africans from their homes and transplanting them into ghetto-like living conditions. Black South Africans received poorer health services, could only attend school to a certain age and for job training. Voting manual rights were severely restricted to prevent the overturn of the white supremacists. The Afrikaners were bullies. Black South Africans suffered multiple human rights violations. Those who attempted to overthrow the white rule were put in jail. Internal resistance and international pressure finally caused the collapse of the oppressive regime. When power returned to Black South Africans, it seems natural that they would retaliate, taking away the Afrikaners' homes and possessions and throwing the perpetrators in jail for crimes against humanity. This did not happen. After all the violence and trauma, the new South African government wanted peace. They sought a unified nation. The Truth and Reconciliation Commission (TRC) was established to ensure a safe and peaceful transition. The functions of the TRC were to investigate the violations of human rights, allow the victims to talk honestly and openly about their suffering, find ways to reconcile the pain and trauma, and to grant amnesty from criminal convictions for the perpetrators in return for telling the truth. The TRC refused to silence the victims. They gave the victims voice, which allowed the healing process to commence. Due to the efforts of the TRC and courageous, wise leaders, South Africa was able to transition into a more equitable nation without further violence and destruction. The TRC is not without criticism. Some people feel that those who committed the human rights violations should not have been given amnesty. The Afrikaners should have been punished. There will always be some people who feel that the best and only way to handle violence is with greater violence. Studying other methods of handling violence may help to educate this group. The TRC model provides a unique and constructive approach for other countries and communities struggling with large-scale social injustices.

The nation has changed since earlier generations. It is no longer acceptable for bullies to walk the hallways of schools, tormenting those who they perceive as undesirable, lesser on their imaginary social hierarchy. Despite more recent efforts to stop bullying, the pain suffered by previous generations still exists. Grandparents, parents, aunts, uncles, and other members of the community do not trust authorities to do the right thing when it comes to bullying. Based on their experiences, bullying still exists. There is no reason for past victims and bystanders to expect anything different when it comes to their son, daughter, niece, nephew, cousin, or grandchild. Institutions that openly allowed bullying, such as schools, police departments, and local governments, cannot expect people to trust and respect them until they are willing to accept responsibility for their past role in victimization. New relationships—relationships based on trust and respect—can only be established through open and honest communication. Institutions can use ideas from truth and reconciliation to repair the broken trust and loss of respect that resulted from generations of unabated bullying. Because of their care for all persons and respected status in society, medical professionals are often in an ideal position to guide the truth and reconciliation process.

Reconciliation is a process of recovery for both the survivor and the offender that is grounded in spiritual practice. Reconciliation does not disregard the past in order to make things right. The process acknowledges the violations of the past, hence the phrase "TRUTH and reconciliation" instead of just "reconciliation." Reconciliation consists of seven steps: realization that reconciliation is a difficult and arduous route, finding a common goal, giving voice to past injustices, healing, putting systems in place that respect the rights of all groups, transformation, and maintenance (Katongole & Rice, 2008). Reconciliation is not an easy, idyllic solution. Reconciliation requires patience, a willingness to speak and listen to horrific injustices, and a desire for a peaceful, just society. Both sides must be willing to give up feelings of entitlement. The injustices, hurts, insults, humiliation, and pain can never be removed, forgotten, or soothed. The community must take time to listen to the feelings and experiences of survivors and to agree that the offenses were real and painful. Moving forward too fast, without allowing sufficient time for the survivor to voice experiences and concerns will interfere with later stages. Both parties must maintain an attitude that, in order to move forward, people must learn from the past. Survivors and offenders must agree to a common goal. In schools that are dealing with the sequelae of generations of bullying, the common goal is building a safe, productive learning community. The goal cannot be silencing the survivors, forgetting the past, or moving on. The goal should be mutual, shared power, with respect for individual differences. After everything is learned about the violations that can possibly be learned, systems must be put in place to ensure that the injustices can never happen again. The WHO report outlines steps toward just, nonviolent communities, including equal access to educational and health services, equal quality of services, equality and justice in the criminal justice system, and social supports for those who are struggling or economically disadvantaged. The community may need to set aside specific days to reflect on the past injustices. Future success of the community depends on the health and wellness of the entire community, not just one, selected portion. Developing a community with social justice requires collaboration. The next step is healing, a time of peace, adjustment, controlled and reserved interactions. Healing requires care for the self, the wounded, and the disenfranchised. Healing allows those who committed the violations to come to terms with their offenses and to experience remorse. Healing requires survivors, offenders, and bystanders to act in ways that model respect and trust. The next step, transformation, occurs without warning. In transformation, it is as if people wake up one morning and find themselves in a different world, a world of acceptance, hospitality, understanding, wisdom, hopes, and dreams. Maintaining this new world requires ongoing care for vulnerable members and vigilance for those who would disrupt it. There may always be people who feel that passivity and acceptance are signs of weakness, a vulnerable group to be conquered. These are the potential bullies, would-be offenders, people who feel that they deserve community resources more than others. The reconciled community must be vigilant for would-be offenders and treat such ignorance with education. True bullying prevention is a never-ending process.

SECTION II

Controversies and Issues

"Victimization Builds Character"

Bullying is an imbalance of power where the bully has power over the victim and is intentionally abusing the power in order to hurt the victim. Some victims can empower themselves to effectively counterbalance the bully's power. Confronting the bully, fighting back, making a safety plan to avoid the bully, telling a friend or adult for intervention, or ignoring verbal attacks are different strategies used by victims. If the chosen strategy is successful, the victim may use the techniques for other abusive interactions, later in life. This gives the impression that the victim has gained character. However, these are rare cases. In many cases, the bully has too much power and the victim is simply unable to counterbalance this power. This is not through any fault or weakness of the victim. It is simply a result of who holds the greatest social power. When the victim is unable to counterbalance the power or is subjected to prolonged, ongoing humiliation or is dealing with other issues, such as divorce in the family, learning disabilities, or chronic illness, the abuse can become a breaking point. Victims report anxiety, low self-esteem, depression, and suicidal and homicidal ideations. Some victims carry the hurt of bullying into adulthood where they have trouble forming and maintaining close, personal friendships. They lose faith in other people's ability to comfort and support them. Some victims may turn into bullies as a way to counteract bullying. For the most part, the adverse social and emotional consequences of bullying victimization do not support the idea that bullying builds character. Victimization may build character for a tiny proportion of the population. However, for most people, bullying is traumatic and painful and not something that should be tacitly approved.

"Telling will Only make it worse"

Bullies hold more social power than victims. So, there are cases where, if the victim reports bullying, the adult will side with the bully and the abuse will get worse. When adults fail to intervene, the bully sees that there are no limits to his or her behavior and will keep abusing the victim. The lack of intervention by adults sends the message that the victim is not important or deserves the abuse, which further hurts the victim. If the adult does nothing or the bullying gets worse, the victim should continue to tell other adults until one adult acts. Someone will eventually see through the bully's excuses and put a stop to it. There are several factors to consider in reporting bullying. First, the adult may actually intervene, but there is the appearance of nonaction because the adult has misperceptions about proper policy and procedures. Some adults feel that they cannot follow up with victims because it would violate confidentiality. They cannot discuss disciplinary actions with a third party. This is a misperception in that there are ways to discuss the safety of the victim without violating confidentiality policy. A second factor is that some early elementary-age children characteristically tell everything to adults. This means that the adults may have information overload, and trouble determining which reports to follow up on. It is developmentally appropriate to ask young children whether they are telling to help or telling to hurt. If the reporter is telling to help the victim, the intent is pro-social and needs attention. If the reporter is telling to hurt the bully, the intent is antisocial and should either be reconsidered or rephrased as a pro-social report. The third factor to consider is that adults are human, with the same flaws, faults, and problems as youth. Not all adults perform their duties with professionalism and integrity. Some teachers may still be resolving their own psychosocial issues of acceptance or nonacceptance when they were young. They may be afraid to stand up to the popular crowd or don't know how to stand up to people with more power. This is why it is important to keep telling one adult after another until someone listens. Eventually, the victim will find a teacher, administrator, or security officer who knows and understands the interpersonal dynamics of bullying, is confident in his or her abilities to stand up to the bully, and can balance professional obligations with school policy.

"Bullies have Low Self-Esteem"

True bullies do not have low self-esteem. Bullies are powerful, confident people, with high social standing (Juvonen, Graham, & Schuster, 2003). Bullies have less depression, social anxiety, and loneliness than victims. In interventions, the high self-esteem will prohibit the bully from recognizing that he or she is causing the problem. The true bully is arrogant, blaming the victim for the abuse. In comparison to bullies and nonvictims, victims have very low self-esteem. This misconception of low self-esteem among bullies may have arisen from observations of provocative victims. Provocative victims are victims who fight back or turn into bullies due to their experiences with chronic victimization. Provocative victims are not true bullies as their actions are usually reactionary, in reaction to abuse or perceptions of abuse by others. Attacks arise out of frustration. Provocative victims are usually genuinely sorry and very remorseful after the attack, a reflection of a realistic or low self-esteem. True bullies have high self-esteem.

"All Bullies are Bad and All Victims are Good"

People prefer to think in simple terms. It is difficult and takes effort to understand the complex interactions that take place during bullying. In an effort to break events down into ways that people can easily understand, the media, investigators, and prosecutors will only present information that supports a good or bad viewpoint. The problem is that this dichotomous view locks us into a mindset that is hard to break through. Humans are much more complex than good or bad. To believe that good people only do good things and bad people do bad things misses the entire essence of human nature and sets up an ideal which is unrealistic. Seeing people as purely good or evil means that the motives of good people go unquestioned and bad people experience severe social injustices. For example, for many decades, some Catholic priests sexually abused children while senior members of the church failed to intervene. The religious persona of the priests put them into the good category, raising their interactions with youth above question. When the victims matured and raised charges of molestation, some of the perpetrating priests were defrocked, those who covered up the abuses were forced to resign, hundreds of millions of dollars were paid out in lawsuits, membership of the Catholic Church suffered, and public support and respect was severely damaged. Raising some people into the good category can be very dangerous. Alternatively, stigmatizing a child as bad can be just as destructive. If an impulsive youth attempts to shoplift, assuming that the child is a chronic thief can be very harmful. Rehabilitation with other offenders could increase criminality. The child would learn more serious shoplifting techniques and social norms would be reset, where the child begins to believe that shoplifting is the norm. In order to protect society, it is important to step out of the mindset that all offenders are bad and all victims are good. People are people with faults, flaws, and needs. Placing one group above question or making assumptions about certain groups is dangerous.

"We don't have any Bullying Here"

An estimated 1.6 million children are bullied at school once a week or more often and an estimated 1.7 million youth report bullying others (U.S. Department of Justice, 2001). Bullying happens in schools, communities, workplaces, anywhere people come together and where one person feels the need to exert power over another person. To claim that there is no bullying in a particular school or community means that the person making the claim is either in denial, clueless, or a bully. Bullying happens everywhere. Over a person's lifetime, there is a 99.9 percent chance that someone, somewhere, will try to bully him or her.

"This Program will Stop All Bullying in a School"

Developing programs for public and private schools is a lucrative business. School administrators regularly receive expensive, flashy brochures promising to solve all of the school's social ills. More pressure comes from parents and local community when program developers convince talk show hosts and television news that their program is effective. School administrators are forced to select programs that are popular, politically beneficial, or agree with the personal philosophies of school board members. The reality is that there is no magic potion to stop bullying. A one-hour program presented by someone who flies in from another community cannot address the specific issues and needs in the target community. The program may be upbeat, stimulating, and thought-provoking, and if the school is lucky, the program may even change students' behavior for the rest of the day. However, students and adults quickly return to their old behaviors and styles of relating. The changed behavior is not reinforced and sustained over time. Some programs may even cause more harm by highlighting differences between students or identifying personal weaknesses, which may set a child up for future victimization. The programs that work are not flashy, pretty, or exciting. Effective programs require hard work, dedication, a personal investment in children, and ongoing support, revision, and reinvestment. The federal government reviews youth violence prevention programs to determine whether they are effective. Programs that are effective are listed on the National Registry of Evidence-Based Programs and Practices (http://www.nrepp.samhsa.gov/), a searchable database of drug and violence prevention programs. Programs not listed have not met the evidence of effectiveness and should only be used secondary to the programs that work.

"We have a Zero Tolerance Policy. We do not Tolerate Bullying"

Zero tolerance has different meanings to different people. Zero tolerance refers to a lack of tolerance for children who bully or a lack of tolerance for bullying behaviors. These two meanings are extremely different in school practice. Zero tolerance for the bully means that adults punish children who bully or children who attempt to bully. Typical punishments are suspension, expulsion, or transfer to another school. School administrators use social exclusion techniques to control undesirable behavior. The problem with ostracizing bullies is that social exclusion is itself a form of bullying. Administrators are modeling an undesirable behavior. Using a form of violence to deal with violence can very counterproductive and may increase violent behaviors, rather than decreasing violent behaviors. Suspending the bully for one to three days is counterproductive to the educational process. Suspension, expulsion, and transfers interfere with learning and increase one of the risk factors for violence—disengagement from the school and community. Suspensions are also contrary to how youth learn. Social learning theory proposes that rewards will increase certain behaviors. Suspension, a mini-vacation of sorts, is a reward. It does not make sense to reward bullies with one to three days off for hurting another youth. Zero tolerance for the bully is a dangerous policy because schools are, unfortunately, a reflection of the larger stereotypes and biases of society. True bullies are usually immune from zero tolerance policies because of their social status within the school. School disciplinarians will harshly punish the child who smells bad, looks different, or gets on everyone's nerves, but will not punish the son or daughter of a local township official, the star athlete, or a member of the popular group of girls. In addition to holding these "get out of jail free" cards, bullies are great manipulators and can easily convince adults that the victim bullied them first or somehow deserved the mistreatment. Thus, zero tolerance policies tend to impact the children who are provocative victims or experimenting with the behavior, not true bullies. Because of the racial, gender, and socioeconomic disparities in school discipline practice, zero tolerance for the bully often means zero tolerance for *some* bullies, not *all* bullies.

Zero tolerance for the behavior is a positive disciplinary approach that stops the undesirable behavior as soon as it occurs. Zero tolerance for the behavior means that teachers, adults, or other bystanders are vigilant for behaviors and intervene to stop the behaviors. Zero tolerance for the behavior is based on theories of how people learn. People learn best when the information is relevant to their current situation or needs. A teachable moment is an unplanned educational opportunity that occurs through natural events. It is a set of circumstances that allows the learner to acquire new values, skills, information, or behavior because the information is directly and immediately relevant to life. For example, if an adult observes a group of children, a potential bullying circle, moving toward a possible target, the adult may say to the group, "Stop. Think about what you are doing." Once the group has had the time to think about their actions, it would be worthwhile to discuss potential motives and ways to avoid future temptations. Teachable moments occur when a child is engaged in the events and can apply the information to the current circumstances. Zero tolerance for the behavior is hard work. It means that the adult must be constantly vigilant for aggressive behaviors, engaged in what the students are doing, willing to speak out when something is not right, and willing to confront potential bullies with respect and dignity. True zero tolerance for bullying behaviors promotes an inclusive, pro-social environment and models appropriate behaviors to children, providing sustained bullying prevention.

"We need more Police Officers in our Schools"

Police officers are not trained in child development or the teenage brain. Police training includes physical training, functions of the criminal justice system, constitutional and criminal laws, criminal procedures, motor vehicle laws, patrol procedures and crisis management, as well as other functions of policing. Police are trained to collect evidence, report, and convict, which means that officers are allowed to use tactics, such as lying, in order to coerce a confession. An estimated 2.3–5.0 percent of people in prison are believed to be innocent (http://www.innocenceproject.org/). This translates to 46,000–100,000 innocent people in prison. There are many reasons for the high numbers of innocent people in jail. Youth are particularly at high risk of false conviction because youth are trained to trust police officers. When youth are interrogated by police, they are often told that it doesn't matter if they admit to the crime. The officer will put in a good word for them. Youths believe the officer and only realize their mistake once they get into the criminal justice system. The police officer is not likely to care whether an innocent person has gone to jail and a guilty person is walking free because, in his or her mind, the youth probably did something, somewhere, sometime, to deserve jail. Children need to be protected from officers who perform shoddy investigations or coerce confessions. One way to protect children is to ensure that people who have access to children in school are trained to understand normal childhood brain development and have the child's best interests at heart. A second issue with having police officers in schools is that police officers may unintentionally increase violence through promoting the weapons effect and modeling gun-carrying in school. The weapons effect is a psychological effect produced by weapons. People exposed to guns act more violently than people not exposed to guns. This means that children at recess will act more violently when they are exposed to someone with a gun, even if the gun is holstered. Some children are naturally attracted to guns. They will ask questions about the gun and show respect to the person carrying the gun. This respect can be misleading to other children, particularly the victim of bullying, who is looking for ways to get respect. The victim may believe that he or she can gain respect by bringing a gun to school. The undeveloped brain does not consider long-term consequences, possibly because there were no adverse consequences to the police officer who brings a gun into school. Many schools have installed panic alarm systems, immediately notifying the local police of a school threat. Police officers, themselves, have questioned the usefulness of these systems. Semiautomatic weapons produce a great number of victims in a very short period of time. The Nickel Mines perpetrator shot 10 victims in eight seconds. Police cannot respond faster than a semiautomatic weapon. The best outcomes in school attacks were handled by teachers or staff who knew the student and were able to bond within the first seconds of the threat. School attacks are best prevented through caring and concerned adults in schools.

"Bullies should be Given a Dose of their Own Medicine"

The idea that hurting children will stop them from hurting other children is contrary to theories of how people learn. Children learn by watching adults. If adults act harshly, aggressively, or violently, children will act violently. Harsh punishment can aggravate attacks if the bully is acting out of frustration. Punishing the hot bully, the child who is bullying out of frustration, is like throwing gasoline on a fire. It will only anger and frustrate the child further. Punishing the cold bully, the child who carefully plans the attacks, will drive the behavior out of sight. If behaviors become more subtle, it is harder for adults to detect bullying, and victims are left unprotected. Punishments can hurt both the bully and the victim. Threat of punishment also does not work. People do not learn in a condition of fear. In order for people to learn, they must be focused on the issue, not on avoiding punishment. A more appropriate term to use when dealing with bullying behaviors is discipline. Punishment and discipline are not synonymous. Punishment is intended to hurt. Discipline is intended to teach. Punishment has a negative connotation. Discipline has a positive connotation. Discipline teaches self-control and mastery. Discipline is hard work because it requires communicating expectations, modeling the behavior, watching to ensure that the learner can perform the skill and perform the skill at the appropriate time and place, and monitoring the behavior or skill for continued improvement. Discipline requires communication, patience, understanding of normal childhood development, care, and compassion. Discipline is not a quick and easy fix, but it does have lifelong impact.

"We just need to Teach Children not to Bully"

Health professionals learned the hard way that telling youth not to do something does not necessarily work. The "Just Say No" campaign was an extensive and expensive antidrug campaign led by First Lady Nancy Reagan in the 1980s. The campaign increased the awareness of drugs as a problem and provided one solution, "Just say no." The problem is that "just say no" is an overly simplistic suggestion. The campaign did not take into account the addictive nature of drugs, the biological and psychological reasons why people use drugs, or youthful curiosity. When people are addicted to drugs, just saying no is insufficient. The campaign did not take into consideration the nature of the teenage brain, to try new things and rebel against authority. The campaign also assumed that knowledge will deter a problem. This is incorrect. Many people know that they should not use drugs and continue to do so. Knowledge is not enough to change behavior. Knowledge must be combined with skills, resources, and a tailored approach that addresses people at different stages of considering, experimenting, using, and addiction to drugs. Public health educators learned a lot from this and other failed antidrug campaigns. The Truth Campaign by the American Legacy Foundation has been a highly successful antismoking campaign. The founders—marketing, advertising, and public health professionals with suggestions from youth—used concepts from marketing to reduce cigarette smoking, a common gateway to illicit substances. The Truth advertisements used real people in startling and dramatic representations and employed popular genres to grab the viewer's attention and convey the antismoking message. Rather that acting as the authority, something that might have backfired with adolescent thinking, the developers portrayed tobacco companies as authorities driving a wedge between tobacco advertising and youth. Multiple studies have demonstrated the effectiveness of the campaign. Unlike the "Just Say No" campaign,

The Truth Campaign struggles for funding. Lessons learned from antismoking campaigns can be directly translated to antiviolence campaigns. Education, alone, is insufficient. In order to stop violence, programs must be developmentally and culturally appropriate, presented and employed by professionals who know and understand normal childhood development, properly funded, and undergo continuous evaluation and improvement.

SECTION III

Resources

Child-Help USA (1-800-4-A-Child or http://www.childhelp.org/) is a national nonprofit organization dedicated to meeting the physical, emotional, and spiritual needs of abused, neglected, and at-risk children in the United States, Canada, the U.S. Virgin Islands, Puerto Rico, and Guam. Child-Help manages a 24-hour hotline, advocates for children, manages residential treatment centers, provides child abuse prevention, education, and training, and increases awareness and healing through the National Day of Hope®.

International Bullying Prevention Association (IBPA) (http://www.stopbullyingworld.org/) is a professional organization designed to support quality research into bullying prevention principles and practices in order to promote a safe learning environment in schools and good citizenship among youth. IBPA serves as a network for professionals in the field of bullying prevention and support for educators and community members.

It Gets Better Project (www.ITGETSBETTER.ORG) is a social movement sending the message to LGBT people that the torment and bullying that they may be experiencing is temporary and the future will be much more positive. The project uses current technology, the Internet, YouTube, and celebrity speakers to provide a supportive community for youth. The website contains a blog to discuss media events, a pledge for advocates, videos, and a posting of events.

National Cyber Security Alliance (NCSA) (www.staysafeonline.org) is a nonprofit organization supported by public and private organizations, such as AT&T, CISCO, EMC², Facebook, Google, McAfee®, Microsoft, PayPal, SAIC®, Symantec™, Verizon, and VISA with the Department of Homeland Security. The organization provides information, tools, and resources for individuals, parents, teachers, and businesses on how to use the Internet safely.

National Suicide Prevention Lifeline (1-800-273-TALK or http://www.suicidepreventionlifeline.org/): The Mental Health Association of New York City manages a 24-hour, toll-free, confidential hotline and website for anyone in the nation considering suicide. The Lifeline routes incoming calls to local crisis centers where emergency counseling and referrals can be made to appropriate organizations.

OnGuard Online (http://onguardonline.gov/) is a joint project by the Naval Criminal Investigative Service, Office of Justice Programs, Federal Deposit Insurance Corporation, Federal Trade Commission, Homeland Security, U.S. Department of Education, and multiple other organizations. The website provides education in order to keep people safe online. OnGuard Online is a partner in the Stop.Think.Connect campaign (http://www.stopthinkconnect.org/), a public service campaign to promote safe Internet usage, shared responsibility, and cybersecurity.

StopBullying.gov (www.stopbullying.gov/) is an official government website managed by the U.S. Department of Health and Human Services in partnership with the Department of Education and the Department of Justice. The site provides excellent information for youth, parents, educators, and community members on how to stop or prevent bullying.

Striving to Reduce Youth Violence Everywhere (STRYVE) (www.safeyouth.gov) is an online resource from the Centers for Disease Control and Prevention (CDC). STRYVE provides information on youth violence definitions and causes, risk and protective factors, extent of the problem, prevention, and community resources.

The Youth Voice Project (www.youthvoiceproject.com) by Stan Davis and Charisse Nixon is a large-scale research project that collects information from youth on what they believe is most helpful in reducing bullying and healing after bullying.

Youth Violence: A Report of the Surgeon General (www.surgeongeneral.gov/library/youthviolence) is a classic resource for researchers studying early findings on best practices in youth violence prevention. The chapters cover introduction to youth violence, extent of the problem, youth developmental factors, risk factors, prevention, and intervention. The report was very controversial in that it presented research demonstrating that some of the most popular programs in youth violence prevention, such as boot camps, Drug Abuse Resistance Education (DARE), and group therapy, do not work and may actually cause more harm than good. The report is a free resource, available online or in print edition.

Measuring Bullying Victimization, Perpetration, and Bystander Experiences: A Compendium of Assessment Tools (2011) is a free resource compiled and edited by M. Hamburger, K. Basile, & A. Vivolo and published by the Centers for Disease Control and Prevention, National Center for Injury Prevention and Control, Division of Violence Prevention. This free resource is a good starting point for those who want to study bullying in their own community. The compendium contains copies of validated surveys from around the world. All surveys are in English. The surveys can be used to discover the extent of bullying in a particular community, to determine what interventions are needed, based on identified problems, or to study the degree of success of a particular program. Using preexisting surveys, such as those provided in this compendium, supports an unbiased, honest view of the problem and allows comparisons with published findings. The current edition contains surveys on aggression for bullies, victimization scales, cyberbullying, school climate surveys, and peer nomination scales (where respondents categorize classmates on particular traits).

Glossary

accident: An event caused by carelessness, ignorance, or misconduct. In health, the term *accident* has been replaced with the term *unintentional injury* in order to convey the idea that these incidents are preventable.

agentic state: A state of the mind that is characterized by blind obedience to authorities. The individual follows leaders without question.

aggression: A forceful action marked by hostility or destructiveness.

altruistic suicide: A subtype of suicide where victims are highly integrated into the social group and believe that the needs of the group are more important than the needs of the individual.

anomic suicide: A subtype of suicide where victims experience sudden life changes that make them feel disconnected from values, traditions, or goals.

antioxidants: Substances that protect the body from potentially harmful chemical reactions. Antioxidants bond with free radicals and protect against cancer, heart disease, and some other health problems.

arousal: A state of being that occurs when the body is physically and mentally prepared to receive or respond to a stimulus.

autonomous state: A condition of the mind when the individual is able to act according to his or her own values, attitudes, beliefs, and free will.

beneficence: The state of doing good through charity or acts of kindness.

best practices: Efforts, programs, or treatments that have been proven, through research studies, to work.

betrayal trauma: The hurt and shock resulting from situations where institutions or people who have a duty to protect others fail in that duty. The person who has not been protected feels violated, distrustful, and loses confidence in the responsible organization.

boele: Sweetheart or lover. The original term from which the word *bully* was derived.

bully: *(noun)*—A person with power who regularly abuses another person with lesser power. *(verb)*—The act of abusing another person with lesser power.

bullycide: To intentionally or unintentionally cause the death of a person through direct or indirect abuse.

bullying: Intentional and chronic abusive behaviors performed by someone with social power.

bully-victim: A person who is both a bully and a victim, also known as provocative victim.

bystander: Someone who witnesses bullying.

bystander effect: A misconception produced when multiple people observe another person in need and fail to help the victim because they assume that others will act.

carcinogen: A poison or toxin that causes cancer.

case study: A type of research study that explores and describes in detail the life experiences of one person or group of people.

causal factor: A factor or condition that determines whether a specific disease, event, or outcome will occur.

causality: An action, condition, or factor that brings about a specific outcome.

coercive power: The ability to control other people or situations through force or threat.

cognitive dissonance: A state of discomfort produced when thoughts, actions, or deeds are not consistent with core beliefs or values.

collaboration: A style of working with other people that involves bringing together people of different strengths and backgrounds in order to achieve a common goal.

companionship: An interpersonal relationship that is characterized by commitment, peace, and sympathy toward one another.

competitive bullying: Bullying for the purpose of obtaining more resources than other people.

competitive style: A style of working that places personal needs and desires before the needs of the group. As one party competes with others, the competitive style can become hostile.

conditions of causality: Scientific standards that must be met in order to determine that a factor produces a specific outcome.

consequences: The result caused by a set of conditions or actions.

cyberbullying: The action of abusing others using Internet technology or other electronic means.

defender: A bystander who acts against bullying to protect the victim.

deindividuation: The loss of independent thought, action, interest, or initiative.

depression: A serious medical condition characterized by feelings of sadness and disinterest. Depression is treated with medication and counseling by mental health specialists.

desensitization: To decrease or extinguish the body's normal responses or feelings to a situation or event.

diagnosis: The act of investigating signs or symptoms in order to identify the cause or disease.

diffusion of responsibility: When an individual feels less responsible for coming to the aid of a person in need because the person assumes that others will act.

disease: A condition that interferes with normal functioning of the human body. *Dis* means "not" and *ease* means "free of pain or burdens." Thus, *dis-ease* means "not free of pain or burdens."

disinhibition: The overcoming of natural instincts or restraints that leads a person to act in ways that he or she would not normally act.

egoistic suicide: A subtype of suicide when victims feel detached or alienated from the social group because they do not share the same values, traditions, attitudes, and goals as others in the group.

enactive learning: A way of gaining knowledge through interaction with the environment.

endemic: Native or natural to a particular geographic region or group of people.

epidemic: Rapid outbreak or growth of a health condition in a specific geographic area or within a specific group of people.

expert power: The ability to control other people or situations through special knowledge, skills, or abilities.

fatalistic suicide: A subtype of suicide in which the victims live in an overly oppressive and abusive society and prefer to die than to live without freedom.

frontal lobe: The part of the brain located in the front of the cerebral hemispheres. The frontal lobe controls emotions and personality.

frustration: A negative emotion, characterized by dissatisfaction and feelings of ineffectiveness.

Genovese syndrome: Also known as *bystander effect*, occurs when an individual or group of individuals fails to help a person who is in need of help.

Golden Rule: A code of ethics that states that a person should treat others in ways that he or she wishes to be treated.

henchman: A highly aggressive member or follower of a gang.

herd behavior: When groups of individuals act in unison without planning or forethought.

homicide: The death of a human being caused by the action or inaction of another person.

incentive: A factor that has the ability to incite action.

indicated prevention: A form of treatment that targets those who already suffer from a health problem and aims to prevent or limit the undesirable consequences of that problem.

injury: Damage to the human body caused by exposure to mechanical, thermal, electrical, chemical, or radiant energy.

intentional injury: Purposeful damage to the body by exposure to mechanical, thermal, electrical, chemical, or radiant energy.

intermittent reinforcement: A type of behavioral reinforcement where a person is periodically given a reward for performing a desired skill. The person does not receive the reward every time the skill is performed.

intervene: To alter a problem, condition. or disease while it is occurring in order to minimize undesirable outcomes.

intervention: Programs, people, or behaviors that alleviate a problem, condition, or disease while it is occurring.

justice: To treat fairly using the principles of truth, fairness, and equality.

laboratory study: A type of research study that tests participants' responses to a stimulus.

legitimate power: The ability to control other people or situations through one's position in society.

malicious: An intent to do wrong or to make another person suffer.

mimicry: Imitating the actions or behaviors of another person.

mobbing: A term for bullying that is now used primarily to describe workplace bullying. Mobbing is when one individual leads other people to repeatedly and intentionally attack one specific individual in the group.

mock bullying: Actions that resemble bullying but lack the intention to harm the other person. Mock bullying refers to incidents that are staged for the purpose of tricking adults into giving rewards to students who act as peacemakers or defenders during bullying incidents.

model: A symbol used to represent a larger or more complex idea or concept.

moderating factor: A factor or condition that affects an individual's potential for disability or disease.

narcissism: Excessive egocentrism that interferes with the person's ability to form healthy relationships.

needs assessment: A systematic investigation of a health problem within a specific population. Needs assessments are used to identify the next steps toward alleviating the problem.

negative reinforcement: The removal of an undesirable experience in order to promote a desired behavior.

observational learning: A way of learning that involves watching others perform the behavior.

paradigm: A clear example, pattern, or model that represents a larger concept.

passive victim: The target of bullying who responds in ways that do not resist the abuse.

positive reinforcement: Giving of a reward in order to increase the likelihood of a certain behavior.

posttraumatic stress disorder (PTSD): A mental health disorder that is triggered by a traumatic or stressful event. People with PTSD experience flashbacks, nightmares, severe anxiety, and distressing and uncontrollable memories of the event.

power: Degree of control over other people or the immediate environment.

practice: The action of improving health. In medicine, medical treatments, radiology, physical therapy, speech therapy, occupational therapy, and surgical procedures are practices.

precipitating event: A factor or condition associated with the onset of a disease or illness.

predatory bullying: Bullying with the intent of exploiting others for personal, emotional, or material gain.

preexisting data: A collection of information that was gathered on previous occasions for other purposes that is later reviewed for new information.

prevalence: The number of people affected by a particular disease or condition divided by the total number of people (affected and unaffected) in the population at the same point in time.

prevention: Programs, people, or behaviors that stop an anticipated event, condition, or disease from occurring.

priming: To prepare someone for a specific reaction by exposing the person to a combination of stimuli, one of which normally produces the desired reaction.

protective factor: A condition that promotes optimal health.

provocative victim: A victim who uses aggression to resist abusive treatment.

pseudo-bullying: Behaviors that mimic bullying except they lack an imbalance of power.

psychosomatic complaints: Physical symptoms of illness that are caused by emotional stress or other mental health disorders.

punishment: A hurtful action inflicted in response to a wrongdoing.

quadriplegic: Paralysis of both arms and both legs.

recall bias: A phenomenon in research where respondents distort events in their mind and report the distorted events as real.

reciprocal violence: When both parties in a relationship act aggressively toward each other.

referent power: The ability to control other people or situations by making people feel special.

relational ethics: A field of ethics that examines the interdependency of human beings in care-giving and care-receiving roles.

respect for persons: The bioethical principle that describes treating others with dignity, kindness, and honor.

reward: An incentive, praise, or gift that is given in return for desired behavior.

reward power: The ability to control other people or situations through incentives, praise, or gifts.

risk factor: A condition that increases the potential for injury or disease.

selected population: People who are at high risk for a particular health problem.

selected prevention: A form of treatment that aims to prevent a health problem among those who are at high risk.

self-harm: The act of injuring oneself through cutting, an overdose of drugs or alcohol, or other harmful behaviors.

sexting: Electronic transmission of sexually explicit material in pictures or messages.

skin conductance: The electrical conductance of skin, used to measure levels of psychological or physical arousal.

Social Cognitive Theory: A theory describing how people learn social behaviors.

sociologist: A scientist who studies the nature and behaviors of people in groups.

somatoform disorders: Physical symptoms, such as headache, stomachache, or backache, that cannot be explained by a disease or injury.

suicide: The intentional act of killing oneself.

symptom: A sign that indicates disease or disorder of the body.

teachable moment: An unplanned incident or event that allows those involved to reflect on the incident in order to gain knowledge.

theory: A hypothetical set of concepts that provide an explanation for complex behaviors, events, or situations.

treatment: The medical or surgical remedy for a health problem.

unintentional injury: Unexpected hurt or damage to the body that results from carelessness, ignorance, or misconduct.

universal population: People who are unaffected or marginally affected by a health problem.

universal prevention: A form of treatment that targets all people in the population, including those who do not suffer from a health problem, and aims to prevent the problem in the population.

vicarious reinforcement: A type of behavioral reinforcement where a person learns a skill by watching other people receive a reward for performing the desired skill.

victim: A person who is intentionally or unintentionally subjected to abuse, mistreatment, or oppression.

violence: The use of physical force or power that either results in physical or emotional injury or has a high likelihood of resulting in injury, death, or psychological harm.

weapons effect: A phenomenon where the visual presence of a firearm causes people to act more aggressively than they normally would.

References

Bandura, Albert. *Social Learning Theory.* Englewood Cliffs, NJ: Prentice-Hall, 1977.

Baranowski, Tom, Cheryl L. Perry, and Guy S. Parcel. "How Individuals, Environments, and Health Behavior Interact." In *Health Behavior and Health Education: Theory, Research, and Practice*, edited by Karen Glanz, F.M. Lewis, and B.K. Rimer, 153–78. San Francisco, CA: Jossey-Bass, 1997.

Barton, Paul E. *One-Third of a Nation: Rising Dropout Rates and Declining Opportunities.* Princeton, NJ: Policy Information Center, Educational Testing Service, 2005.

Beck, Aaron T. *Prisoners of Hate: The Cognitive Basis of Anger, Hostility, and Violence*. New York: HarperCollins, 1999.

Berkowitz, Leonard. *Aggression: It's Causes, Consequences, and Control.* Philadelphia, PA: Temple University Press, 1993.

Berkowitz, Leonard, and A. LePage. "Weapons as an Aggression-Eliciting Stimuli." *Journal of Personality and Social Psychology,* 7, no. 2 (1967): 202–207.

Black, Sally, Ericka Washington, Vernard Trent, Patricia Harner, and Ericka Pollock. "Translating the Olweus Bullying Prevention Program into Real World Practice." *Health Promotion Practice*, 11, no. 5 (2010): 733–40.

Black, Sally, Dan Weinles, and Ericka Jackson. "Victim Responses to Bullying, Perceptions of What Works, What Doesn't." Scientific Proceedings at 2007 AERA Conference, Chicago, IL, 2007.

Blumer, Dietrich, and D. Benson. "Personality Changes with Frontal and Temporal Lesions." In *Psychiatric Aspects of Neurologic Diseases,* edited by D. Frank Benson and D. Blumer. New York: Grune & Stratton, 1975.

Broidy, Lisa M., Richard E. Tremblay, Bobby Brame, D. Fergusson, John, L. Horwood, Robert Laird, Terrie E. Moffitt, Daniel S. Nagin, John E. Bates, Kenneth A. Dodge, Rolf Loeber, Donald R. Lynam, Gregory S. Pettit, and Frank Vitaro. "Developmental Trajectories of Childhood Disruptive Behaviors and

Adolescent Delinquency: A Six-Site, Cross-National Study." *Developmental Psychology* 39, no. 2 (2003): 222–45.

Brunner, Han G., M. Nelen, X. O. Breakefield, H. H. Ropers, and B. A. van Oost. "Abnormal Behavior Associated with a Point Mutation in the Structural Gene for Monoamine Oxidase A." *Science* 262, no. 5133 (1993): 578–80.

Buckley, Jerry. "The Tragedy in Room 108." U.S. News & World Report, http://www.usnews.com/usnews/news/articles/931108/archive_016061_4.htm.

Bureau of Justice Statistics. "Alcohol and Crime: Data from 2002–2008." Office of Justice Programs (2010), http://bjs.ojp.usdoj.gov/content/acf/29_prisoners_and_alcoholuse.cfm.

Cairns, Robert B., M.-C. Leung, and B. D. Cairns. "Social Networks over Time and Space in Adolescence." In *Pathways through Adolescence: Individual Development in Relation to Social Contexts,* edited by Lisa J. Crockett and Ann C. Crouter, 35–56. *The Penn State Series on Child and Adolescent Development.* Hillsdale, NJ: Erlbaum, 1995.

Centers for Disease Control and Prevention. Updated 2009. "Youth Risk Behavior Surveillance—United States Surveillance Summaries." MMWR 2010; 59 (N. SS-5).

Children's Defense Fund. *School Suspensions: Are They Helping Children?* Cambridge, MA: Washington Research Project, 1975.

Coccaro, Emil F., C. S. Bergeman, Richard J. Kavoussi, and A. D. Seroczynski. "Heritability of Aggression and Irritability: A Twin Study of the Buss-Durkee Aggression Scales in Adult Male Subjects." *Biological Psychiatry* 41, no. 3 (1997): 273–84.

Conti-Ramsden, Gina, and Nicola Botting. "Social Difficulties and Victimization in Children with SLI at 11 Years of Age." *Journal of Speech, Language and Hearing Research* 47, no. 1 (2004): 145–61.

Copeland, Mary Ellen. "Building Self-Esteem: A Self-Help Guide." United States Department of Health and Human Services, Substance Abuse and Mental Health Services Administration & Center for Mental Health Services, Rockville, MD, 2002.

Coser, Lewis A. *Continuities in the Study of Social Conflict.* New York: New York Free Press, 1967.

Darley, John M., and Bibb Latané. "Bystander Intervention in Emergencies: Diffusion of Responsibility." *Journal of Personality and Social Psychology* 8, no. 4 (1968): 377–83.

Davis, Stan, and Julia Davis. *Schools Where Everyone Belongs: Practical Strategies for Reducing Bullying.* Champaign, IL: Research Press, 2007.

Diener, Edward. "Effects of Prior Destructive Behavior, Anonymity, and Group Presence on Deindividuation and Aggression." *Journal of Personality and Social Psychology* 33, no. 5 (1976): 497–507.

Dollard, John, Leonard W. Doob, Neal E. Miller, O. H. Mowrer, and Robert R. Sears. *Frustration and Aggression.* New Haven, CT: Yale University Press, 1939.

Eiden, Rina D., Jamie M. Ostriv, Craig R. Colder, Kenneth E. Leonard, Ellen P. Edwards, and Toni Orrange-Torchia. "Parent Alcohol Problems and Peer Bullying and Victimization: Child Gender and Toddler Attachment Security as Moderators." *Journal of Clinical Child & Adolescent Psychology* 39, no. 2 (2010): 341–50.

Eron, Leonard D., Jacquelyn H. Gentry, and Peggy Schlegel (eds.). *Reason to Hope: A Psychosocial Perspective on Violence & Youth.* Washington, DC: American Psychological Association, 1994.

Evans, Patricia. *The Verbally Abusive Relationship: How to Recognize It and How to Respond.* Cincinnati, OH: Adams Media, 2010.

Farrington, David P., and Maria M. Ttofi. "School-Based Programs to Reduce Bullying and Victimization." Systematic reviews for the Campbell Collaboration Crime and Justice Group, 2010, http//www.ncjrs.gov/pdffiles1/nij/grants/229377.pdf.

Faul, Mark, Likang Xu, Marlena M. Wald, and Victor G. Coronado. Traumatic Brain Injury in the United States: Emergency Department Visits, Hospitalizations and Deaths 2002–2006. Atlanta, GA: Centers for Disease Control and Prevention, National Center for Injury Prevention and Control, 2010.

Festinger, Leon, Albert Pepitone, and Theodore M. Newcomb. "Some Consequences of De-Individuation in a Group." *The Journal of Abnormal and Social Psychology* 47, no. 2 (1952): 382–89.

Fitzpatrick, Kevin M., and Janet P. Boldizar. "The Prevalence and Consequences of Exposure to Violence among African American Youth." *Journal of the American Academy of Child and Adolescent Psychiatry* 32, no. 2 (1993): 424–30.

Fleming, Missy, and Kelly J. Towey (eds.). *Educational Forum on Adolescent Health: Youth Bullying*. Chicago, IL: American Medical Association, May 2002.

Fletcher, Anne C., David R. Troutman, Kenneth Gruber, Emily Long, and Andrea G. Hunter. "Context and Closure in Children's Friendships: Prevalence and Demographic Variation." *Journal of School and Personal Relationships* 23, no. 4 (2006): 609–27.

French, John R. P., Jr., and Bertram Raven. "The Bases of Social Power." In *Group Dynamics,* edited by Dorwin Cartwright and Alvin Frederick Zander, 607–23. New York: Harper and Row, 1960.

Freyd, Jennifer J. "Betrayal Trauma." In *Encyclopedia of Psychological Trauma,* edited by Gilbert Ryes, Jon D. Elhai, and Julian D. Ford, 76. New York: John Wiley & Sons, 2008.

Frick, Paul J., and Essi Viding. "Antisocial Behavior from a Developmental Psychopathology Perspective." *Development and Psychopathology* 21, no. 4 (2009): 1111–31.

Gansberg, Martin. "Thirty-Eight Who Saw Murder Didn't Call the Police." *The New York Times,* March 27, 1964.

Gellert, George. A. *Confronting Violence: Answers to Questions about the Epidemic Destroying America's Homes and Communities*. Washington, DC: American Public Health Association, 2002.

Ginsburg, Kenneth R., and Martha M. Jablow. "Building Resilience in Children and Teens." American Academy of Pediatrics, 2006.

Goodwin, Wade. "Beating Charges Split LA. Town along Racial Lines." National Public Radio, 2007, http://www.npr.org/templates/story/story.php?storyId=12353776.

Griffiths, I.J., D. Wolke, A.S. Page, and J.P. Horwood. "Obesity and Bullying: Different Effects for Boys and Girls." *Archives of Disease in Childhood* 91, no. 2 (2006): 121–25.

Hamburger, Merle, Kathleen C. Basile, and Alana M. Vivolo (eds.). *Measuring Bullying Victimization, Perpetration, and Bystander Experiences: A Compendium of Assessment Tools*. Atlanta, GA: Centers for Disease Control and Prevention, National Center for Injury Prevention and Control, 2011.

Harvey, Michael, Darren C. Treadway, and Joyce T. Heames. "The Occurrence of Bullying in Global Organizations: A Model and Issues Associated with Social/Emotional Contagion." *Journal of Applied Social Psychology* 37, no. 11 (2007): 2576–99.

Hennekins, Charles H. and Julia E. Buring. *Epidemiology in Medicine*. Edited by S.L. Mayrent. Boston, MA: Little, Brown and Company, 1987.

Hoover, John H., and Ronald Oliver. *The Bullying Prevention Handbook: A Guide for Principals, Teachers, and Counselors*. Bloomington, IN: National Education Service, 1996.

Horne, Arthur M., Jennifer L. Stoddard, and Christopher D. Bell. *A Parent's Guide to Understanding and Responding to Bullying: The Bully Busters Approach*. Champaign, IL: Research Press, 2008.

Huesmann, L. Rowell. "The Impact of Electronic Media Violence: Scientific Theory and Research." *Journal of Adolescent Health* 41 (2007): s6–s13.

Hughes, Thomas. *Tom Brown's Schooldays*. London: Macmillan, 1857.

Janson, Gregory R., and Richard J. Hazler. "Trauma Reactions of Bystanders and Victims to Repetitive Abuse Experiences." *Violence & Victims* 19, no. 2 (2004): 239–55.

Josephson Institute of Ethics. "The Ethics of American Youth," 2010, http://charactercounts.org/programs/reportcard/2010/installment01_report-card_bullying-youth-violence.html.

Karch, Debra L., Linda L. Dahlberg, and Nimesh Patel. "Surveillance for Violent Deaths—National Violent Death Reporting System, 16 States, 2007." *Morbidity and Mortality Weekly Report,* no. 59 (SS04) (2010): 1–50.

Katongole, Emmanuel, and Chris Rice. *Reconciling All Things: A Christian Vision for Justice, Peace, and Healing*. Chicago, IL: InterVarsity, 2008.

Kim, Jong S., S. Choi, S. U. Kwon, and Y. S. Seo. "Inability to Control Anger or Aggression after Stroke." *Neurology* 58, no. 7 (2002): 1106–8.

Kohlberg, Lawrence. *Stages in the Development of Moral Thought and Action*. New York: Holt, Rinehart & Winston, 1969.

"Konrad Lorenz—Autobiography," http://nobelprize.org/nobel_prizes/medicine/laureates/1973/lorenz.html.

Kosciw, Joseph G., Emily A. Greytak, Elizabeth M. Diaz, and Mark J. Bartkiewicz. *The 2009 National School Climate Survey: The Experiences of Lesbian, Gay, Bisexual and Transgender Youth in Our Nation's Schools*. New York: GLSEN, 2010.

Krug, Etienne G., Linda L. Dahlberg, Anthony B. Zwi, and Rafael Lozano. *World Report on Violence and Health*. Geneva: World Health Organization, 2002.

Kübler-Ross, Elizabeth. *On Death and Dying*. New York: Scribner, 1969.

Lahteenmaki, P.M., J. Huostila, S. Hinkka, and T.T. Salmi. "Childhood Cancer Patients at School." *European Journal of Cancer* 38, no. 9 (2002): 1227–40.

Levinger, George. "Development and Change." In *Close Relationships,* edited by Harold H. Kelley, et al., 315–59. New York: W.H. Freeman and Company, 1983.

Levy, David A., and Paul R. Nail. "Contagion: A Theoretical and Empirical Review and Reconceptualization." *Genetic, Social, and General Psychology Monographs* 119, no. 2 (1993): 233–84.

Loeber, Rolf, and Magda Stouthamer-Loeber. "Development of Juvenile Aggression and Violence." *American Psychologist* 53, no. 2 (1998): 242–59.

Lorenz, Konrad. *Evolution and Modification of Behavior.* Chicago, IL: The University of Chicago Press, 1965.

Lorenz, Konrad. *On Aggression.* New York: Bantam Books, 1966.

Lutgen-Sandvik, Pamela. "Take This Job and . . . Quitting and Other Forms of Resistance to Workplace Bullying." *Communication Monographs* 73, no. 4 (2006): 406–33.

Lyketsos, Constantine G., Oscar Lopez, Beverly Jones, Annette L. Fitzpatrick, John Breitner, and Steven DeKosky. "Prevalence of Neuropsychiatric Symptoms in Dementia and Mild Cognitive Impairment: Results from the Cardiovascular Health Study." *JAMA* 288, no. 12 (2002): 1475–83.

Manuck, Stephen B., Janine D. Flory, Robert E. Ferrell, Karin M. Dent, J. John Mann, and Matthew F. Muldoon. "Aggression and Anger-Related Traits Associated with a Polymorphism of the Tryptophan Hydroxylase Gene." *Biological Psychiatry* 45, no. 5 (1999): 603–14.

Marsee, Monica A., and Paul J. Frick. "Exploring the Cognitive and Emotional Correlates to Proactive and Reactive Aggression in a Sample of Detained Girls." *Journal of Abnormal Psychology* 35, no. 6 (2007): 969–81.

McKenna, M., Hawk, E., Mullen, J., and Hertz, M. "Bullying among Middle School Students in Massachusetts." *JAMA* 305, no. 22 (2009): 2283–86.

Merriam-Webster.com. "Bully," 2011, http://www.merriam-webster.com/dictionary/bully.

Milgram, Stanley. "Behavioral Study of Obedience." *Journal of Abnormal and Social Psychology* 67, no. 4 (1963): 371–80.

Moeller, Thomas G. *Youth Aggression and Violence: A Psychological Approach.* Mahwah, NJ: Lawrence Erlbaum Associates, 2001.

Moffitt, Terrie E. "Adolescence-Limited and Life-Course-Persistent Antisocial Behavior; a Developmental Taxonomy." *Psychological Review* 100, no. 4 (1993): 674–701.

Nansel, Tonja R., Mary Overpeck, Ramani S. Pilla, W. June Ruan, Bruce Simons-Morton, and Peter Scheidt. "Bullying Behaviors among U.S. Youth: Prevalence and Association with Psychosocial Adjustment." *Journal of the American Medical Association* 285, no. 16 (2001): 2094–100.

NCES. *Digest of Education Statistics*, 2008, http://nces.ed.gov/programs/digest/d08/tables/dt08_160.asp.

Nelson, Randy J. (ed.). Biology of Aggression, Oxford: Oxford University Press, 2006.

New Jersey Department of the Public Advocate and Division of Mental Health Advocacy. *College Students in Crisis: Preventing Campus Suicides and Protecting Civil Rights.* Trenton, NJ, 2009.

Nordhagen, Rannvieg, Nielsen, A., Stigum, H., and Köhler, L. "Parental Reported Bullying among Nordic Children: A Population-Based Study." *Child: Care, Health and Development* 31 (2005): 693–701.

O'Farrell, Timothy J., William Fals-Stewart, Marie Murphy, and Christopher M. Murphy. "Partner Violence before and after Individually Based Alcoholism Treatment for Male Alcoholic Patients." *Journal of Consulting and Clinical Psychology* 71, no. 1 (2003): 92–102.

Olweus, Dan. "Aggression and Hormones: Behavioral Relationships with Testosterone and Adrenaline." In *Development of Antisocial and Prosocial Behavior: Research, Theories, and Issues,* edited by Dan Olweus, Jack Block, and Marian Radke-Yarrow, 51–72. Orlando, FL: Academic Press, Inc., 1986.

Olweus, Dan. *Bullying at School: What We Know and What We Can Do.* Cambridge, MA: Blackwell, 1993.

Olweus, Dan. "A Profile of Bullying at School." *Educational Leadership* 60 (2003): 12–18.

Olweus, Dan, and Limber, Susan. *Blueprints for Violence Prevention: Book Nine: Bullying Prevention Program.* Golden, CO: Venture Publishing; Denver, CO: C & M Press, 2000.

Pereznieto, P., Harper, C., Clench, B., and Coarasa, J. "The Economic Impact of School Violence: A Report for Plan International." London: Overseas Development Institute, 2010, http://plan-international.org/files/global/publications/campaigns/Economic%20Impact%20of%20Scool%20Violence%20ODI-Plan%20Oct%202010.pdf.

Perkins, H. Wesley, Jessica M. Perkins, and David W. Craig. "Where Does Bullying Take Place among Adolescents When They Are at School?" Paper presented at the American Public Health Association Annual Meeting, Philadelphia, PA, 2009.

Phillips, Rick. "The Financial Costs of Bullying, Violence and Vandalism," http://www.nassp.org/Content.aspxtopic=The_Financial_Costs_of_Bullying_Violence_and_Vandalism_Web_only_.

Phillips, Rick, John Linney, and Chris Pack. *Safe School Ambassadors: Harnessing Student Power to Stop Bullying and Violence.* San Francisco, CA: Jossey-Bass, 2008.

Pinheiro, Paulo Sérgio. *World Report on Violence against Children.* Geneva: UN, 2006.

Pontegal, Michael, Gerhard Stemmler, and Charles Spielberger. *International Handbook of Anger: Constituent and Concomitant Biological, Psychological, and Social Processes.* New York: Springer, 2010.

Reilly, Patrick M., and Michael S. Shropshire. *Anger Management for Substance Abuse and Mental Health Clients: A Cognitive Behavioral Therapy Manual.* Rockville, MD: Center for Substance Abuse Treatment, Substance Abuse and Mental Health Services Administration, 2002.

Reiss, Albert J., Jr., and Jeffrey A. Roth (eds.). *Understanding and Preventing Violence.* Vol. 1. Washington, DC: National Academy Press, 1993.

Roland, Erling, and David Galloway. "Professional Cultures in Schools with High and Low Rates of Bullying." *School Effectiveness and School Improvement* 15, no. 3–4 (2004): 241.

Rosenberg, Mark L., and Mary Ann Fenley (eds.). *Violence in America: A Public Health Approach.* New York: Oxford University Press, 1991.

Russell, Stephen T., and Kara Joyner. "Adolescent Sexual Orientation and Suicide Risk." *American Journal of Public Health* 91, no. 8 (2001): 1276–81.

Schwab-Stone, Mary E., Tim S. Ayers, Wesley Kasprow, Charlene Voyce, C. Barone, T. Shriver, and R. P. Weissberg. "No Safe Haven: A Study of Violence Exposure in an Urban Community." *Journal of the American Academy of Child and Adolescent Psychiatry* 34, no. 10 (1995): 1343–52.

Selye, Hans. *The Stress of Life.* New York: McGraw-Hill, 1956.

Shapiro, Alan. "Jena and It's Tree of 'Ignorance.'" Morningside Center for Teaching Social Responsibility, 2007, http://www.teachablemoment.org/high/jena.html.

Sharp, Sonia, and Peter K. Smith. *Tackling Bullying in School: A Practical Guide for Teachers.* London: Routledge, 1994.

Skiba, Russel J., Robert S. Michael, Abra Carroll Nardo, and Reece L. Peterson. "The Color of Discipline: Sources of Racial and Gender Disproportionality in School Punishment." Research Report #SRS1. Indiana: Indiana Education Policy Center, 2006.

Song, Li-yu, Mark I. Singer, and Trina M. Anglin. "Violence Exposure and Emotional Trauma as Contributors to Adolescents' Violent Behaviors." *Archives of Pediatrics and Adolescent Medicine* 152, no. 6 (1998): 531–36.

Strandmark, K. Margaretha, and Lillemor R.-M. Hallberg. "The Origin of Workplace Bullying: Experiences from the Perspective of Bully Victims in the Public Service Sector." *Journal of Nursing Management* 15, no. 3 (2007): 332–41.

Substance Abuse and Mental Health Services Administration. "15+ Make Time to Listen, Take Time to Talk . . . About Bullying. Conversation Starter Cards," 2008, http:store.samhsa.gov/product/15-Make-Time-To-Listen-Take-Time-To-Talk-About-Bullying/SMA08–4321.

Sutherland, E.H., Donald R. Cressey, and David F. Luckenbill. *Principles of Criminology.* 4th ed. Chicago, IL: Lippincott, 1939.

Tsafos, Amanda, Sally Black, and Ericka Washington. "A Tailored Mental Health Approach to Bullying Interventions." Pennsylvania Public Health Association Annual Conference, November 17–19, Philadelphia, Pennsylvania, 2008.

Twemlow, Stuart W., and Frank Sacco, "The Prejudices of Everyday Life, with Observations from Field Trials." In *The Future of Prejudice: Psychoanalysis and the Prevention of Prejudice,* edited by Henri Parens, A. Mahfouz, S. W. Twemlow, and D. E. Scharff, 237–54. Lanham, MD: Jason Aronson, 2007.

U.S. Department of Education. *Truancy: A Serious Problem for Students, Schools, and Society,* n.d., www2.ed.gov/admins/lead/safety/training/truancy/problem_pg17.html.

U.S. Department of Health and Human Services. *Youth Violence: A Report of the Surgeon General.* Rockville, MD: U.S. Department of Health and Human

Services, Centers for Disease Control and Prevention, National Center for Injury Prevention and Control; Substance Abuse and Mental Health Services Administration, Center for Mental Health Services; and National Institutes of Health, National Institute of Mental Health, 2001.

U.S. Department of Justice. *Addressing the Problem of Juvenile Bullying* (Vol. OJJDP fact sheet #27). Washington, DC: Author, 2001.

United States Public Health Service. *National Strategy for Suicide Prevention: Goals and Objectives for Action.* Washington, DC: United States Public Health Service, 2001.

Van Cleave, J., and Davis, M. M. "Bullying and Peer Victimization among Children with Special Health Care Needs." *Pediatrics* 118, no. 4 (2006): e1212–e1219.

Virginia Tech Review Panel. "Mass Shootings at Virginia Tech: Report of the Review Panel," 2007, http://www.governor.virginia.gov/TempContent/tech PanelReport.cfm.

Vossekuil, Bryan, Robert A. Fein, Marisa Reddy, Randy Borum, and William Modzeleski. "The Final Report and Findings of the Safe School Initiative: Implications for the Prevention of School Attacks in the United States." U.S. Department of Education, Office of Elementary and Secondary Education, Safe and Drug-Free Schools Program and the U.S. Secret Service, National Threat Assessment Center, Washington, DC, 2002.

Warner, Rebecca L., Gary R. Lee, and Janet Lee. "Social Organization, Spousal Resources, and Marital Power: A Cross-Cultural Study." *Journal of Marriage and the Family* 48, no. 1 (1986): 121–28.

Wheeler, Ladd. "Toward a Theory of Behavioral Contagion." *Psychological Review* 73, no. 2 (1966): 179–92.

Willard, Nancy. "Cyberbullying & Cyberthreats: Responding to the Challenge of Electronic Aggression." Center for Safe and Responsible Internet Use, 2009, http://www.ippvid.org/conference/willard_cyberbulling_handout.pdf.

Williams, Kirk R., and Nancy G. Guerra. "Prevalence and Predictors of Internet Bullying." *Journal of Adolescent Health* 41, ed. 6, suppl. 1 (2009): S14–S21.

Wolak, Janis, Kimberly J. Mitchell, and David Finkelhor. "Does Online Harassment Constitute Bullying? An Exploration of Online Harassment by Known Peers and Online-Only Contacts." *Journal of Adolescent Health* 41, ed. 6, suppl. 1 (2007): S51–S58.

World Health Organization. *World Report on Violence and Health,* edited by E. G. Krug, L. L. Dahlberg, J. A. Mercy. Geneva: World Health Organization, 2002.

World Health Organization. *International Statistical Classification of Diseases and Related Health Problems, Tenth Revision*, no. 2(19). Geneva: World Health Organization, 2004.

INDEX

Acceptance stage of loss, 99
Adolescents: brain development, 79–80, 113–14, 138; bullying by, 79; emotional and hormonal changes, 79; importance of "referent power," 36; Pathway Models of understanding, 80–81; self-doubt of, 36; suicides, 25–26. *See also* School attacks
"All bullies are bad and all victims are good," 133–34
American Academy of Pediatrics (AAP), 121
Amish community, 20–21, 124
Anger stage of loss, 97–98
Atlantic Shores Christian School attack (Virginia), 18
Attacks, forms of: coercive bullying, 32–33, 37; cyber bullying, 43–44, 123; e-mail bullying, 23, 43; emotional bullying, 32, 35, 40–46, 64–65, 100; mock bullying, 39; nonverbal bullying, 42–44; physical bullying, 4, 19, 42–43, 48–49, 64; psychological bullying, 44–46; verbal bullying, 4, 6, 18–19, 28–29, 35, 39, 42–46; workplace bullying, 38–39, 45–46, 93
Attention deficit hyperactivity disorder (ADHD), 4, 7, 50
Attractiveness, 36–37
Austria, bullying rates, 47
Authority conflict, violence-related pathway (Pathway Model), 80

Bandura, Albert, 11, 12, 71, 82, 118, 135. *See also* Social Cognitive Theory
Bethel Regional High School attack, 19
Betrayal trauma, 66
Biological causes of bullying, 74–77
Bobo Doll learning experiments (Bandura), 12
Brain: adolescent development, 79–80, 113–14, 138; and aggressive behaviors, 74; consequences of victimization, 63–65; development in adolescence, 79; and facial asymmetry, 37; neurological changes, 5; survival

function, 61; traumatic brain injuries, 37, 74–75; and traumatic brain injury, 75
Brampton Centennial Secondary School attack (Canada), 18
Bullies: coercive bullies, 32–33, 37; forms of attack by, 32–33, 35, 37, 39–40, 42–46, 123; and imbalance of power, 32–38; incongruent relating styles of, 86–88; offender services for, 105–6; suffering of, 4; symptoms of perpetration, 59–62. *See also* Causes of bullying; Henchmen of bullies; School attacks
"Bullies have low self-esteem," 132–33
"Bullies should be given a dose of their own medicine," 137–38
Bully, term derivation, 12–13
Bullying, causes of, 71–94; adolescent development, 79–81; being a henchman of a bully, 88–89; biological, 74–77; community factors, 93–94; frustration leading to aggression, 77–78; Genovese syndrome, 89–91; incongruent relating styles, 86–88; institutionalized bullying, 91–93; moral development, 83–86; narcissistic personality, 78–79; violence as a learned behavior, 81–93
Bullying Prevention Program (BPP), 14–15, 120
Bully Police, 27, 122–23
Bulwer-Lytton, Edward, 35
Burning behavior, 3, 58
Bystander Effect, 90–91. *See also* Genovese syndrome
Bystanders to bullying: health related consequences, 68–69; joining attack with bullies, 26; passivity of, 10; power imbalance influence, 32; roles of, 41–42; traumatization of, 3–4, 6–8; victim support by, 109. *See also* Henchmen of bullies

California Department of Rehabilitation, 52–53
Canada, bullying data, 3–4
Carneal, Michael, 19–20
Causes of bullying. *See* Bullying, causes of
Center for Independent Living, 52–53
Center for Mental Health Services, 120
Centers for Disease Control, 120, 145
Child-Help USA, 143
Children: with alcoholic parents, 76; bulling vs. maltreatment, 40; consequences of witnessing bullying, 68–69; disabled children, 49, 52; egotistic, narcissistic behavior of, 78–79; empathy developed by, 79; friendless children, 49; gay male children, 51; gender ambiguity children, 51; health consequences of bullying, 4–5; and imbalances of power, 32–38; impact of exposure to violence, 71–72; lesbian children, 51; mentally challenged children, 49; obese children, 50; rights to safety, 15, 55; and Social Cognitive Theory, 82–83; special needs children, 50; suicide hangings, 25–29; symptoms of being bullied, 55–59; TBI risk factors, 74; twin studies, 75–76; victimization of, 55–59; violence studies, 11–12;

vulnerabilities of, 15–16. *See also* School attacks
Cho, Seung-Hui, 23–24
Civil rights movements, 32
Coercive bullying, 32–33, 37
Columbine High School attack, 8, 21
Community-level influences of bullying, 4, 93–94
Computerized Axial Tomography (CAT) scans, 63–64
Conditions of causality (defined), 71
Connected Kids: Safe, Strong, Secure program, 121
Covert violence-related behavior (Pathway Model), 80
Culture of Violence Theory, 93–94
Cutting behavior, 3, 28, 58
Cyber bullying, 43–44, 123

Dating violence, 3, 15, 23, 37–39, 66–67
Defenders of bullying, 42
Denial stage of loss, 97
Denmark, bullying rates, 47
Depression of bullies, 66, 132–33. *See also* Cho, Seung-Hui
Depression of victims: assessment of victims, 64; and brain damage, 75; causes of, 4, 6, 57, 63, 131; identification and treatment of, 119, 122; long-term effects, 131; self-destructive behaviors of, 58; signs of, 57; as stage of loss, 97–98; and suicide, 59; treatment of, 119. *See also* High, Jared; Loukaitis, Barry; Meier, Megan; Suicide
Diagnosis of bullying: bully vs. victim determination, 55; perpetration symptoms, 59–62; victimization symptoms, 55–59
Disabled children, as victims, 49, 52
Disengaged onlookers, 41–42
Documentation of attacks, 101
Drug abuse, 4
Drug Abuse Resistance Education (DARE), 144
Durkheim, Emile, 24
Dyslexia, 7

Educators role in bullying prevention: appropriate handling of bullying incidents, 116–19; classroom management, 115–16; evidence-based programs, 120–21; threat assessment, 119–20
Egotistic behavior of children, 78–79
Elderly people, 74, 102
Elliot, Nicholas, 18, 20
E-mail bullying, 23, 43
Emergency medical care, 96–97
Emotional bullying, 32, 35, 40–46, 64–65, 100
Emotional health, 6
Emotional support for victims of bullying, 97–99
Empathy building strategies, 106–9
Endemic bullying, 5
England, bullying rates, 47
Epilepsy, 7
Evidence-based prevention programs, 120–21

Facial structure, 37
False rumors, 6
Follower henchmen, 41
French, John R. P., Jr., 32
Friendless children, as victims, 49
Friendships: development strategy, 102–5, 111; feigning of, 50, 102; mock friendships, 88; school administration support, 115; struggles of victims with, 36
Frontier Middle School attack (Washington), 18–19

Gay male children, as victims, 51
Gender ambiguity children, as victims, 51
Genetics: and aggressive behavior, 74, 76; behavioral studies, 75–77; and criminality, 82; twin studies, 75–76; violence studies, 15
Genovese, Kitty, 89–91
Genovese syndrome, 89–91
Germany, bullying rates, 47
Global bullying rates, 47
Good boy/nice girl morality (of moral judgment), 84–85
Great Britain, bullying data, 3–4
Greece, bullying rates, 47
Greenland, bullying rates, 47

Hanging suicides
Hanging suicides by students: Carl Hoover, 25; Jaheem Herrera, 25; Jessica Logan, 27–28; Megan Meier, 25–26; Montana Lance, 28; Phoebe Prince, 28–29
Harris, Eric, 21
Harry Potter (Rowling), 12
Health High School attack (Kentucky), 19–20
Health-related consequences, 63–70; assessment modalities, 63–64; and betrayal trauma, 66; of combined victimization and perpetration, 68; hormonal reactions, 64–65; nervous system reactions, 65; of perpetrators, 66–67; and trauma theory, 65–66; of victims, 63–66; of witnessing bullying, 68–69
Heinemann, Peter Paul, 12
Henchmen of bullies: follower henchmen, 41; and herd behavior, 10, 81; reasons for becoming, 88–89; recruitment of by bullies, 43, 45; supporter henchmen, 26, 41–42, 57, 83, 89. *See also* Bystanders to bullying
Herrera, Jaheem, 25
High, Jared, 25–26
High-risk groups, 49–53
HIV/AIDS, risk factors, 66–67
Homicide, 3
Hoover, Carl Joseph Walker, 25
Hurricane Katrina, bystander effect and, 91

Incongruent relating styles, of bullies, 86–88
Instant messaging, 43
Institutionalized bullying, 91–93
Intellectual health, 6
International Bullying Prevention Association (IBPA), 143
Intimate Partner Violence (IPV), 39–40
It Gets Better Project, 143

Japan, bullying data, 3–4

King, Martin Luther, Jr., 35
Kohlberg, Lawrence, 84–86. *See also* Moral judgment stages
Kübler-Ross, Elizabeth, 97, 99

Lance, Montana, 28
Law and order orientation (of moral judgment), 85
Laws against bullying, 122–27; Bully Police USA criteria, 122–23; individual states, 123; truth and reconciliation commissions, 124–27; WHO recommendations, 123–24
Lesbian, gay, bisexual, or transgendered (LGBT) youth, as victims, 49, 51, 53, 143
Lesbian children, as victims, 51
Limber, Susan, 14–15
Literary examples of bullying, 12
Lithuania, bullying rates, 47

Logan, Jessica, 27–28
Lorenz, Konrad, 9–11
Losses, stages of, 97–99
Loukaitis, Barry, 18–19, 20

Magnetic Resonance Imaging (MRI) studies, 64
Measuring Bullying Victimization, Perpetration, and Bystander Experiences: A Compendium of Assessment Tools (ed. Hamburger, Basile, Vivolo), 144–45
Meier, Megan, 25–26
Mental Health Association of New York City, 144
Mentally challenged children, as victims, 49
Mock bullying, 39
Moral judgment stages (Kohlberg): good boy/nice girl morality, 84–85; law and order orientation, 85; naïve hedonistic or instrumental orientation, 84; obedience/punishment orientation, 84; social contract orientation, 85; universal ethical principle orientation, 85–86
Motivators, internal and external, 33, 35

Naïve hedonistic or instrumental orientation (of moral judgment), 84
Name-calling, 4, 6, 19, 28, 39, 43, 48–49, 112, 117
Narcissistic behavior of children, 78–79
Nasty rumors, 4, 28, 34, 37, 45, 49
National Center for Injury Prevention and Control, 120, 145
National Cyber Security Alliance (NCSA), 143
National Institute of Mental Health, 120
National Institutes of Health, 120
National Registry of Evidence-Based Programs and Practices, 120
National Suicide Prevention Lifeline, 144
Naval Criminal Investigative Service, 144
Nazi Germany, 10, 12, 88, 91, 94
Negative reinforcement, 33–34
Newcomers in school, as victims, 50
Nonverbal bullying, 42–44
Northern Ireland, bullying rates, 47
Norwegian bullying study, 12–14

Obedience/punishment orientation (of moral judgment), 84
Obese children, as victims, 50
Offender services for bullies, 105–6
Olweus, Daniel, 13–15, 41. *See also* Bullying Prevention Program
Olweus Bullying Prevention Program (BPP), 14–15, 120–21
OnGuard Online, 144
Overt violence-related behavior (Pathway Model), 80

Parental role in bullying prevention: discussions of bullying and behavior expectations, 110–11; friendship building support, 111; limiting exposure to media violence, 113–14; prevention of violence-related behaviors, 111–12; restricting access to firearms, 113
Passive supporters to bullying, 41, 45
Passive victims of bullying, 56
Pathway Models, of understanding adolescent identity development, 80–81
Pearl High School attack (Mississippi), 19
Pediatric health care providers, 121–22

Pennington, Gary Scott, 18
Perpetration of bullying, symptoms of, 59–62
Physical bullying, 4, 19, 42–43, 48–49, 64
Physical health, 6
Positive reinforcement, 33, 41
Possible defenders of bullying, 42
Power imbalances, 31–38. *See also* Referent power; Reward power
Prevalence of bullying, 47–53; age and gender differences, 48; high-risk groups, 49–53
Prevention strategies, 99–101
Prince, Phoebe, 28–29
Provocative victims of bullying: bullying of others by, 60; characteristics of, 56, 68, 77, 133; children with special health needs, 50; guilt, shame, embarrassment of, 107; mental health of, 68; prevalence rates, 47; zero tolerance policy impact on, 135
Psychiatric disorders, 4, 18, 23, 50, 66
Psychological consequences of bullying: burning behavior, 3, 58; cutting behavior, 3, 28, 58; schizophrenia, 63–64; substance abuse, 25, 63. *See also* Depression of victims
Psychologically/psychiatry challenged people, as victims, 50

Racial prejudice studies (Heinemann), 12
Ramsey, Evan, 19
Raven, Bertram, 32
Referent power, 32, 36–38
Research methods for studying bullying: field studies, 8; intervention studies, 9; laboratory studies, 8–9; surveys and public records, 7–8
Research studies, historical background: Bullying Prevention Program, 14–15, 120; herding studies, 9–11; mobbing studies, 9–12; Norwegian bullying study, 12–14; stereotypes and racial prejudice studies, 12; suicide and peer abuse study, 12; violence and learning studies, 11–12
Respect based on appearance, 36–37
Reward power, 32–34
Richland School attack (Tennessee), 18
Road rage, 3
Roberts, Charles Carl, IV, 20
Roberts, Ed, 51–53
Rouse, James Ellison, 18
Rumors: false rumors, 6; nasty rumors, 4, 28, 34, 37, 45, 49
Rwanda genocide, bystander effect and, 91

School attacks: Bath Consolidated School, 17; causative factors, 18–20; Cleveland Elementary School, 17–18; Columbine High School, 8, 21; consequences for perpetrators, 18–20; Enoch Brown School Massacre, 16; financial consequences of bullying, 69–70; Jena High School, Louisiana, 93; Virginia Tech massacre, 23–24. *See also* Educators role in bullying prevention
Self-mutilation: burning behavior, 3, 58; cutting behavior, 3, 28, 58
Sexually transmitted diseases (STDs), 66–67
Slobodian, Michael, 18
SNERTS ("Snotty nosed egotistical rude teenagers"), 100

Social Cognitive Theory (SCT; Bandura), 12, 71, 82, 118, 135
Social contract orientation (of moral judgment), 85
Social health, 6–7
South Africa Truth and Reconciliation Commission, 124–25
Special needs children, as victims, 50
Spiritual health, 7
Stereotype studies (Heinemann), 12
StopBullying.gov, 144
Striving to Reduce Youth Violence Everywhere (STRYVE), 144
Student hanging suicides, 25–29
Substance Abuse and Mental Health Services Administration, 120
Suicide: bullying association, 4, 12, 16, 24–30; by car bombing, 17; hanging suicides, 25–29; Native American rate, 24; by perpetrators of violence, 18–19, 21–23; U.S. deaths, ranking, 3, 12, 21
Supporter henchmen, 41, 89
Sutherland, Edwin, 81–82
Sweden, bullying rates, 47
Switzerland, bullying rates, 47
Symmetry of features, 36–37

TBI. *See* traumatic brain injury
"Telling will only make it worse," 132
Text messages, 43
"This program will stop all bullying in a school," 134–35
Tom Brown's Schooldays (Hughes), 12
Trauma theory, 65–66
Traumatic brain injury (TBI), 37, 74–75
Treatment and prevention: attack prevention, 99–101; building empathy, 106–9; bystander support for victims, 109; educator's role, 115–21; emergency medical care, 96–97; emotional support of victims, 97–99; laws, 122–27; offender services, 105–6; parental role, 110–14; pediatric health care providers role, 121–22; post-trauma healing, 102; supportive friendships, 102–5
Truth and Reconciliation Commission (TRC), 124–25
Twins, studies of, 75–76

United States (U.S.): bullying data, 3–4; bullying rates, 47; death from injuries data, 3
Universal ethical principle orientation (of moral judgment), 85–86
U.S. Department of Health and Human Services, 120
U.S. Secret Service, 22

Verbal bullying, 4, 6, 18–19, 28–29, 35, 39, 42–46
Vicarious reinforcement, 34
"Victimization builds character," 131
Victims/victimization: attacks at school, 16–24; bully vs. victim determination, 55; coercive bullying, 32–33, 37; comparison with nonvictims, 13–14; consequences for, 4; cyber bullying, 43–44, 123; differences by age and gender, 48; emotional bullying, 32, 35, 40–46, 64–65, 100; emotional support for, 97–99; health-related consequences, 63–66; high-risk groups, 49–53; methods of identification of, 5; nonverbal bullying, 42–44; passive victims, 56; perpetration of bullying combined with, 68; physical bullying, 4, 19, 43, 48–49, 64; research studies, 7–8, 13–16; sadness

and depression of, 6; spiritual health consequences, 7; strategies for attack prevention, 99–101; suicide of, 24–30; support of bystanders, 109; symptoms of, 55–59; verbal bullying, 4, 6, 18–19, 28–29, 35, 39, 42–46; workplace bullying, 38–39, 45–46, 93. *See also* Provocative victims of bullying

Violence: authority conflict, violence-related pathway, 80; children's exposure to, 71–72; children's studies, 11–12; covert violence-related behavior, 80–81; Culture of Violence Theory, 93–94; dating violence, 3, 15, 23, 37–39, 66–67; death-related, 3; family-level risk factors, 73; Intimate Partner Violence, 39–40; as a learned behavior, 81–93; overt violence-related behavior, 80–81; Striving to Reduce Youth Violence Everywhere, 144; suicide by perpetrators of, 18–19, 21–23; types of, 3. *See also* Pathway Models, of understanding adolescent identity development

Virginia Polytechnic Institute massacre, 23–24

"We don't have any bullying here," 134

"We have a zero tolerance policy. We do not tolerate bullying," 135–36

"We just need to teach children not to bully," 138–39

"We need more police officers in our schools," 136–37

West Nickel Mines Schoolhouse (Pennsylvania), 20–21

Witnessing bullying. *See* Bystanders to bullying

Woodham, Luke, 19, 20

Workplace bullying, 38–39, 45–46, 93

World Health Organization (WHO): bullying among 13-year olds study, 47–48; definition of health, 5–7; laws against bullying recommendations, 123–24

Youth Violence: Report of the Surgeon General, 120, 144

Youth Violence Project, 144

About the Author

Sally Kuykendall, PhD, is chair and associate professor in the Health Services Department at Saint Joseph's University, Philadelphia, PA. She has worked as a critical care nurse in the United States and abroad, caring for survivors of intentional and unintentional injuries. Kuykendall's study of bullying started with an evaluation of the Olweus Bullying Prevention Program, a position where she met with teachers, parents, and administrators and observed children's behavior at lunch and recess. Her best education in bullying prevention stems from her experiences as a mother of three sons and two stepdaughters.